VOL.4
JOURNAL OF ARMORED
ASSAULT
&
HELIBORNE WARFARE
AF334144

Editor: James R. Hill
Copyright © 2003
by CONCORD PUBLICATIONS CO.
603-609 Castle Peak Road
Kong Nam Industrial Building
10/F, B1, Tsuen Wan
New Territories, Hong Kong
www.concord-publications.com

We welcome authors who can help expand our range of books. If you would like to submit material, please feel free to contact us.

We are always on the look-out for new, unpublished photos for this series. If you have photos or slides or information you feel may be useful to future volumes, please send them to us for possible future publication. Full photo credits will be given upon publication.

ISBN 962-361-070-X
printed in Hong Kong

P.3

Victory Strike
American Helicopters on the Warpath
Yves Debay

P.14

Wiesel
Germany's Airmobile Weapon Platform

Carl Schulze

P.38

Spanish Mechanized Division
"Brunete" N° 1
Yves Debay

Victory Strike
American Helicopters on the Warpath

Yves Debay

The FARP is a rearming station. It takes about 30 minutes to replenish an Apache's arsenal of Hellfire missiles, Hydra rockets and 30mm ammunition.

There is no doubt that the world entered a new phase of its history after 11 September 2001. Although the events of that day can be interpreted in different ways depending on whether one is American, European or Muslem, the consequences of that sinister attack on the World Trade Center and the Pentagon will certainly influence world geopolitics for years to come.

Without these considerations on their minds, but with a certain fury in their hearts, the men and women of the US Army train very hard. They know they are the cogs in the most tremendous war machine that ever existed. For more than a year they have been preparing for a fight, confident that their cause is just. Among them are the pilots and crews of the helicopters of the 12th Aviation Brigade and the 11th Aviation Regiment (Attack Helicopter Regiment, or AHR) which are part of V Army Corps based in Germany. The 11th Attack Helicopter Regiment is doubtless one of the most powerful units in the American arsenal because it has just been equipped with the latest model Apache AH-64D.

Instantly recognizable, the AH-64D "Longbow" has its radar located above the main rotor. Major Max Blumenfeld, public affairs officer of V Corps, explains: "The 11th Attack Helicopter Regiment is made to create havoc in the enemy's rear. Don't forget that during the first Gulf War, it was the Apache that opened the 'fiesta' by destroying Iraqi radar, which allowed the Air Force to launch its assaults. The Apache AH-64 As attached to the division have a different mission because they support the M-1 Abrams and the M-2 Bradleys on the front lines, whereas the 'Deltas' attached to the Corps take care of the second echelon of enemy forces."

It is with this idea in mind that Exercise "Victory Strike III" was held last autumn in the Drawsko Pomorskie region of Poland.

The tactical concept is a simple one: Create a friendly "bubble" more than 200 km (125 miles) deep within enemy territory with the help of the helicopter forces. On paper, the tremendous assets of the US Army allow for such a concept to become a reality. Objectives situated at a farther distance of 400 to 600 km (250 to 370 miles) can be taken care of by the Air Force or the US Navy (sorties launched from aircraft carriers or Tomahawk missiles launched from submarines, or a combination of both)."We can even bring MLRS [Multiple Launch Rocket System] by C-17," confides a staff officer, "and combine their power of saturation with the precision firepower of the Apache."

Most of the American servicemen involved in Victory Strike III are aware that this exercise is, in fact, an enormous rehearsal to test the support units of the Corps in case there is a war with Iraq. The "Delta" Apache "Longbows", which recently arrived in Europe, are the big stars of the exercise.

The 11th Attack Helicopter Regiment, which is based at Illesheim near Wurzburg, includes a staff, two battalions of combat helicopters (2/6 CAV with 22 AH-64As and the 6/6 CAV with 21 AH-64Ds), and a maintenance battalion, the 7/159 Combat Support Group. One can easily imagine the destructive power that would be unleashed if the 43 Apaches were to raid an enemy's logistic parks.

For Victory Strike, the 11th Attack Helicopter Regiment left behind the 2/6 CAV to integrate "Alpha" Apaches of the 1/501 Attack Helicopter Battalion, which is the attack helicopter battalion of the 1st Armored

Designed mainly for air assault and support missions, the UH-60 Black Hawk is also the workhorse of US aviation. It can be employed as a medium lift and transport helicopter. The Chinook is the classic transport helicopter of the US Army.

Division "Old Ironsides". Added to this were four Mi-24 Polish "Hind" helicopters of the 56th Attack Helicopter Regiment. The "Hinds" and "Alphas" played the part of the bad guys, whose task it was to interfere in the operations led by the choppers of the 6/6 CAV.

Compared with its predecessor, the "Delta" operates in a considerably wider battle zone. The "Delta's" striking range remains classified, but a comparison can be drawn between the M-60 tank and the M-1 tank. A platoon of four M-1s can control an area that requires a squadron of 12 M-60s to handle.

The difference lies mainly in that famous ball situated on the rotor. Named FCAR (Fire Control Air Radar), it provides the crew with a complete overall view of the battlefield. This system is coupled with the TADS (Target Acquisition Designation Sight), which is associated with the night vision goggles of pilots' PNVS (Pilot Night Vision System). This makes the "Longbow" one of the most sophisticated helicopters in the world. In case of engagement, the Apache's tracking device can select from 37 different targets, 16 of which can be handled right away. Added to this are detection radar, an auto-pilot system, an alert detector, and navigation radar not present on the "Alpha."

Military observers have noted that in 1999 the US army did not engage its Apaches in Kosovo. The crash of two of the machines, which resulted in the death of the four crewmembers, reduced the intervention

A CH-47D Chinook of the 7/159 Aviation Regiment and a UH-60L of the 3/158 Aviation Battalion fly in formation during Exercise "Victory Strike III". The 7/159 and the 3/158 are both units in the 12th Aviation Brigade, one of the aviation groups participating in the V Corps – Poland joint exercise. The Polish government permitted low-altitude flying over a 200-square-kilometer area of terrain during the exercise.

A UH-60L Black Hawk belonging to the 3/158 "Storm Riders" soars over the Polish countryside. This unit is the strongest aviation battalion in the US Amy.

The versatile Black Hawk can transport 11 fully equipped air assault soldiers along with its crew. It is specifically built to survive small-arms fire.

A UH-60L Black Hawk lifts a Humvee during Victory Strike. In case of war with Iraq, Black Hawks will help to create a large pocket behind enemy lines.

One good turn deserves another. A Humvee tows a UH-60 Black Hawk while it is on the ground.

capacity of units equipped with the Apache. The non-commitment of Apaches in Kosovo was probably based on two factors: 1) an intact Yugoslav anti-aircraft defense system that was effective against low-altitude aircraft and 2) a lack of training of the pilots in Germany. (One cannot conduct a war with the goal of zero deaths under these conditions.) The poor training of the pilots prompted American military leaders to ask Poland, a new member of NATO, to set aside vast sections of its territory so that pilots can push the limits of their aircraft without being restricted (as they are in Germany) to strict environmental constraints. During Victory Strike III, the government in Warsaw authorized nighttime flights at very low altitude over more than 200 square kilometers of its country.

The favorable reputation of the Apache was restored in Afghanistan in March of 2002 when Apaches of the 101st Air Assault Division were called upon as a last resort to help disengage a rifle company belonging to the 10th Mountain Division that was surrounded by elements of Al Qaida. During a fight that lasted for two days, five Apache AH-64As fought non-stop, setting down only long enough to load and deliver provisions and to rearm. The precision of their firing prevented the Islamic extremists from annihilating a company that had had 28 of its men wounded during its helicopter drop. While preventing another Mogadishu-like tragedy, these Apaches were heavily damaged by ground fire, including a direct hit by an RPG-7. Happily, the rocket apparently failed to explode.

The organization of the aviation battalion can vary depending on the units it contains. Generally, there is a command and control company with three "choppers", three combat companies (Alpha, Bravo and Charlie) with six helicopters each, and Delta Company, which is tasked with maintenance and logistics. Within each combat company, the Apaches work in two groups of three, covering each other just like foot soldiers do.

Logistics is one of the strong points of American units, and it is certainly the case with the 11th Attack Helicopter Regiment. The re-supplying of units mostly takes place close to the front lines . . . and sometimes beyond. Victory Strike III was an opportunity for the author to

Prominent in this photo is the nose art of a CH-47D of Foxtrot Co., 7/159 Avn Rgt that was attached to the task force deployed to Poland. The "159" is the heavy lift helicopter unit of V Corps. In Afghanistan, the CH-47D performed better than the Black Hawk in the mountainous environment.

The badge of the 12th Aviation Brigade is displayed on a sign outside the brigade's HQ.

During Victory Strike III, a detachment of six Mi-24 "Hind" helicopters was attached to the US task force. The six Hinds were used to portray enemy helicopters in the joint exercise.

As an AH-64D Apache touches down, a camouflaged Mi-24 from the Polish 56th Attack Helicopter Regiment sits in the background.

visit a FARP (Forward Arming and Refueling Point), a mobile service station combined with an ammunition re-supply point. Radio coded "BP", "SHELL", "ESSO", or "CHEVRON", the FARP is situated ten kilometers (six miles) behind the front line, well within the range of enemy artillery. (In theory, the Apaches have already neutralized the guns!) Lieutenant Sutton of "D" Troop, HQ 6/6 CAV welcomes us to a totally isolated corner of Poland. A lonely UH-60 Black Hawk loaded with spare parts sits near four Oshkosh trucks, each carrying 7000 liters (24,000 gallons) of fuel.

The FARP unit consists of 27 people, each apparently stimulated by an *esprit de corps* as high as that encountered in the 82nd Airborne. A staff sergeant from the Bronx directly oversees provisioning operations. "'D' Troop consists of 27 people, 15 lads in charge of the fuel – seven for the armament and two for maintenance. By radio we learned that an Apache was having problems with vibration, and that explains the presence of the Black Hawk. We do not even transport our own spare parts.

" Five kilometers (three miles) from our position," he continues, "the helicopter pilot warned of his approach and indicated the quantity of 'Coke' he needed. Hoses were pulled from the fuel tanks and six gas pumps were created. In time of war, the number can be increased to eight. The refueling of an Apache takes about 10 minutes and its total rearmament can be done in thirty."

The explanations of the staff sergeant are interrupted by the noise of

a rotor. In the setting sun, six aircraft flying at tree level appear one in front of the other. The soldiers of "D" Troop rush toward the tremendous "war animals", which are refueled with their rotors still turning. "Normally, in time of peace," the sergeant explains, "we stop the rotors for safety reasons, but since September 11, we are at war!"

These helicopters are Apache AH-64As of the 12/501 Attack Helicopter Regiment.

The front view of the Mi-24 Hind in the foreground in this photo shows the machine's short weapon-carrying wings. A typical weapons configuration could include AT-6 air-to-ground missiles and 57mm rocket pods. The Mi-24 Hind was designed to be an assault transport and gunship, but it is versatile enough to fulfill other missions. Its unique appearance is in stark contrast to that of the US helicopters.

The 1/501 AHR is the organic helicopter battalion of the 1st Armored Division "Old Ironsides".

The Apache "Alpha", the AH-64A, lacks the radar ball above its main rotor that is the highly recognizable trademark of the "Delta" version.

During Exercise "Victory Strike III", the AH-64As of the 1/501 were attached to the 11th Attack Helicopter Regiment to stand in for the missing 2/6 CAV. They are not part of the unit.

Here a pilot shows how he would be fastened to a rescue Apache if his machine were to be shot down.

radar, air control and even a sanitary evacuation unit capable of setting up ten field platforms for "choppers" in the middle of nowhere.

Like almost all the units of the US Army, since the autumn of 2001, the 12th Aviation Brigade has undergone extensive training. One month after Exercise "Lighting Storm" in Germany, all of the brigade was in Poland, with the transport and assault helicopters being tasked with creating a friendly "bubble" from which the Apaches can strike deep into enemy territory. In a matter of weeks, the job is likely to be repeated in the sands of the Middle East.

Nearby, Lieutenant Sutton, the leader of the detachment, insures that everything goes smoothly. His combat dress is decorated with paratrooper instructor wings and the helicopter pilot badge. A combat patch worn on his left shoulder is that of the Rangers. "It may surprise you," says Sutton, "but I was part of the Special Forces. I even operated in Africa. It is no mistake that I am in the fuel service. In the US Army, logistics is an elite unit, which is different from the military culture of old Europe."

A FARP can be set up behind enemy lines with the aid of the other helicopter unit of V Corps, the 12th Aviation Brigade. A Chinook from the 12th can also carry soft fuel tanks inside or slung underneath the aircraft. The "fat cow", as the Chinook is called when equipped with fuel, can serve as a mobile service station. Once it lands it can refuel four Apaches at the same time.

The 12th Aviation Brigade consists of two aviation battalions, the 5/158 Aviation Battalion and the 3/158 Aviation Battalion. The 3/158, with its effective force of 840 people, is the most powerful aviation battalion in the US Army. Based at Giebelstadt east of Frankfurt, the 3/158 "Storm Riders" includes two companies: Alpha "Blue Stars" and Bravo "Catfish", each of which has three platoons of five UH-60L Black Hawks. "Delta" Company, the "Rebels", is tasked with maintenance. Also found within the organic unit are the CH-47D Chinooks of Foxtrot Company "Big Windy" with its 16 machines that were obtained from the 7/159 Avn Rgt. For Victory Strike, the 5/158 Avn Bn is equipped with 24 UH-60As, the early less powerful version of the Black Hawk. The 3/58 Aviation Regiment is the brigade's operational support unit. It consists of various units including

A technician performs important maintenance work on the engine of an AH-64 Apache helicopter. The Apache is fitted with two 1690-horsepower T700-GE-701 Turboshaft engines.

A formidable new AH-64D "Longbow" Apache hovers over a landing zone at the Drawsko Pomorskie training grounds.

Exercise "Victory Strike III" was the first operational sortie for the Apache "Delta" stationed in Europe. The Apache is a versatile machine capable of destroying a wide range of targets, including armored vehicles, in all kinds of weather, day or night.

This photograph provides a good view of the large fire control air radar (FCAR) ball that is located above the main rotor, the feature that makes the Apache "Delta" so easy to recognize.

This Apache crew were photographed just after their return from a mission. Every soldier participating in Victory Strike III is aware that his next operation might just be a real war!

The Apache helicopter can be armed with laser-designated Hellfire missiles, a 30mm cannon and Hydra 70 rockets. With its advanced target acquisition system, it is a formidable assault weapon.

Much of the maintenance work performed on AH-64 Apaches is made easier through the help of electronics.

An AH-64D Apache of the 11th Attack Helicopter Regiment touches down at a Forward Arming and Refueling Point (FARP). The refueling of an Apache helicopter is a critically important and potentially dangerous task. The personnel that have this duty are highly trained and capable.

Positioned about 10 kilometers (6 miles) from front lines, the FARP is a kind of temporary service station that enables the Apache pilots to refuel and rearm without being away from their deep-strike mission for too long. If a refueling operation is performed efficiently, it only takes from 10 to 15 minutes for an Apache to be gassed up and sent on its way.

During time of peace, the refueling of an Apache is done only after the helicopter's rotors are no longer turning. Since 11 September 2001, however, a state of war has existed, so the rotors remain spinning. A pilot is usually assigned to the support platoon of an aviation squadron since he knows the needs of the "chopper" pilots landing at a FARP.

This FARP, which has been set up in the pasturelands of Poland, is code-named "ESSO" after the petroleum company. Soldiers from "D" Troop, Headquarters and Headquarters Troop of 6/6th Cavalry man the refueling point.

The AH-64D "Longbows" are the focal point of the V Corps-Polish Exercise "Victory Strike III". They would be unable to fulfill their critical deep-strike missions behind enemy lines if it were not for the efficient re-supply service offered by the support platoon at a FARP.

Just visible through the windshield of this Apache is the unique warthog design on the helmet worn by a crewmember.

A Polish sunset creates a striking silhouette of an Apache "D", probably one of the most sophisticated weapons in the world.

This fuel tanker version of an Oshkosh 8x8 HEMTT (Heavy Mobility Tactical Truck) belongs to "D" Troop of the HQ of 6/6 CAV.

Although Victory Strike III was mainly a heliborne operation, some ground troops were involved in the exercise.

The opening phase of Victory Strike III began with the airdrop of 140 paratroopers of the 173rd Infantry Brigade (Airborne). The paras were dropped from four C-130 Hercules aircraft. The entire operation was directed from Frankfurt, 600 km (373 miles) away from the air base at Miroslawiec, which was the objective.

This Pathfinder officer was in charge on the ground to mark the DZ (drop zone) and authorize the jump.

The appearance of this US paratrooper is typical of the men of the 173rd Infantry Brigade (Airborne) who took part in Victory Strike III. He carries one of a number of versions of the M4 Carbine.

After completing their jump, paratroopers from the 173rd Infantry Brigade (Airborne) regroup to attack the air base at Miroslawiec.

Camouflaged with the surrounding terrain, a paratrooper armed with a carbine fitted with a M203 40mm grenade launcher keeps his eye out for trouble prior to moving on to the next objective.

The paratroops from the 173rd Infantry Brigade (Airborne) encounter some small-arms fire as they advance on the air base.

As the paratroops approached the Miroslawiec air base, they encountered a number of "enemy" troops. When captured, prisoners were quickly searched.

A paratrooper carrying a 5.56mm M249 LMG squad automatic weapon (SAW) pauses near a wall to assess the situation and scan the area for OPFOR (opposing force) troops.

The paratroopers of the 173rd Infantry Brigade (Airborne) are part of US Army Europe's Southern European Task Force. The Polish airfield where they are training is a long way from their home base in Vicenza, Italy.

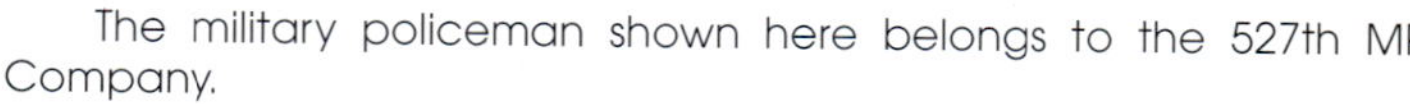

The military policeman shown here belongs to the 527th MP Company.

A water purification station operated by the 240th Quartermaster Company is the source of indispensable drinking water issued to the participants of Victory Strike III. Thanks to the new Water Packaging System, drinking water can be created from water drawn from lakes and streams, as well as salt water. Through a reverse osmosis system, 7,500 gallons of drinking water can be created each hour.

Members of the NBC company of the Polish 1st Corps assemble to participate in a decontamination exercise.

The M270 MLRS is also known as the SPLL (Self-Propelled, Loader/Launcher). This mobile rocket-launching unit provides long-range artillery support for ground troops. It is deadly effective against both personnel and armor.

This image gives a good idea of the clothing worn and the equipment used by the troops tasked with decontamination. Victory Strike III provided an excellent opportunity to practice NBC operations.

After the water is purified and made ready to drink, it is packaged in 1-liter pouches at a rate of 25 pouches per minute. The ability to hydrate troops whenever and wherever needed is a remarkable logistic achievement.

A US MLRS (Multiple Launch Rocket System) belonging to the 1/27 Field Artillery is decontaminated with the help of a Polish WUS-3 truck.

Wiesel

Germany's Airmobile Weapon Platform

Carl Schulze

The Wiesel 1 is used in two variants in the German army and both can be seen in this picture. The one in the foreground is a Wiesel 1 Mk 20mm and behind it is a Wiesel 1 TOW. Both vehicles belong to 5th Company, the heavy company of *Jägerbataillon* 371. The Wiesel 1 Mk 20mm has a crew of two soldiers, a driver and a commander, while the Wiesel 1 TOW has a crew of three soldiers – the driver, commander and loader.

The main advantages of airborne and airmobile forces are their light equipment and the possibility of deploying them to nearly any place in the world without the restrictions faced on the ground. In addition, the deployment can be done in a very short time, and when the troops parachute in or are brought into action by helicopters, there is no need for

an airport in the operational area. Modern airborne forces are trained to deal with a huge range of scenarios. These may include the tasks of forming an entry force for a larger scale operation; seizing bridges or key ground in offensive operations in a wartime scenario; working as a rescue force to save non-combatants trapped in a civil war scenario; deploying as an implementation force in order to divide warring factions during a peace-support scenario; operating as flank protection in a large-scale operation in a conventional war; or deploying behind enemy lines to cut off enemy lines of communications. Whatever scenario facing the airborne or airmobile force, once deployed on the ground the mobility and the availability of heavy weapons is restricted. Unless enough transport vehicles can be seized on the ground, the paratroopers' mobility is limited to the distance they can reach on foot. In addition, the ability to conduct reconnaissance is limited. The paratroopers' heavy weapons that were parachuted in also remain static, which deprives the force commander of the ability to react to a moving battle.

Nicknamed "Garfield", this Wiesel 1 Mk 20mm belongs to the heavy company of *Gebirgsjägerbataillon* 571. The main armament of the vehicle is the Rheinmetall 20mm machine cannon Rh 202 DM 6 mounted in the KUKA-designed E6-II-A1 one-man turret. The turret can be traversed manually 55° to the left and right, and the 20mm cannon has an elevation from −10° to 45°. The 20mm Rheinmetall machine cannon Rh 202 DM 6 has an effective range of 1500 meters (1640 yards) against ground targets and can fire single rounds or bursts.

Since the introduction of airborne and airmobile forces, armies have used a variety of vehicles that could be dropped by parachute or landed by helicopter, but most of these lacked sufficient armor protection and made their crews vulnerable to enemy fire. In 1989, the German army introduced the Wiesel 1 airmobile weapon platform to cope with these restrictions in order to provide its airborne and light infantry units with a light, highly mobile, air transportable, parachute droppable, armored weapon platform. Since then the Wiesel 1 concept has been further developed, and now the German army is on its way to introducing the Wiesel 2, an extended version of the Wiesel 1. This article will review the versions of the Wiesel 1 and 2 that have already been delivered and provide a brief overview of the planned versions, i.e., ambulance, infantry section vehicle, mortar carrier, engineer section vehicle, and reconnaissance vehicle.

Here a Wiesel 1 Mk 20mm participates in a live firing exercise. The 20mm Rheinmetall machine cannon Rh 202 DM can fire single rounds or bursts, as is shown here. The theoretical rate of fire of the machine cannon is 950 rounds per minute. The weapon has a combat range of up to 1500 meters (1640 yards) against ground targets and 1200 meters (1312 yards) against aircraft. The combat range differs slightly depending on the ammunition used. For example, when armor-piercing rounds are used against light armored vehicles, the range drops to 1000 meters (1093 yards).

The Wiesel 1 was designed as an airmobile weapon platform. One of the design requirements for the developing process was the possibility of transporting two Wiesel 1s inside one CH-53G medium transport helicopter. This goal was achieved since the CH-53G has a total payload of seven tons and the Wiesel 1's combat weight is 2.8 tons. Length, height and width were also designed to coincide with the load capacities of the CH-53G. Here a Wiesel 1 Mk 20mm of *Jägerlehrbataillon* 353 exits the interior of a CH-53G during a demonstration held at the German army's infantry school in Hammelburg.

Wiesel 1 – A New Dimension in Airborne Force Mobility

When the Wiesel 1 TOW (Tube-launched, Optically tracked, Wire-command-link guided missile) and Mk 20mm weapon carriers were first issued to the German *Fallschirmjäger* in 1989 to replace the KraKa wheeled airmobile vehicle, and with the *Heeresstrukturreform* 5 (reform of the army structure) in each *Luftlandebrigade* (airborne brigade), one *Fallschirmpanzerabwehrbataillon* (airborne anti-tank battalion) was formed. The main advantages of the Wiesel in comparison to the KraKa are its good cross-country mobility, small silhouette, high speed, and the protection it provides against artillery fragments and small arms fire. This enables the German airborne troops to not only seize an objective after being dropped and hold it until relieved by advancing ground forces, but to react quickly to changing situations.

Before the Wiesel 1 entered service, airborne troops had only limited

The crew of a Wiesel hastily repairs their damaged vehicle after it threw its track during a live firing exercise in Sennelager. The Wiesel belongs to *Fallschirmpanzerabwehrbataillon* 272. Clearly visible is the Diehl Type 622 double-pin track that replaced the older, wire-lined rubber band track. Note the live TOW missile strapped to the hull of the Wiesel 1 TOW.

The highlight of the training exercise for the Wiesel 1 TOW crew is the live firing. Due to the high costs of live missiles, each weapon carrier crew is issued only three missiles per year for training purposes. Before being allowed to fire live missiles, the crew members train for several hours with simulators, following moving targets with lasers. The *Bundeswehr* uses the TOW 2 missile with the HEAT warhead. The minimum effective range of the missile is 65 meters (71 yards), while the maximum range is 3750 meters (4100 yards). The TOW is able to penetrate all armor-protection systems and materials currently in use.

Here a CH-53G of *Heeresfliegerregiment* 35 lifts a Wiesel 1 TOW of *Fallschirmpanzerabwehrbataillon* 262 as an underslung load. In the German army, transporting a Wiesel as an internal load is preferred to underslung loads, because the maneuverability and handling of the helicopter is better. That method also provides a lower flight profile. The underslung technique is used to evacuate damaged vehicles from minefields and transport them back to the field workshop, or when the ground does not allow the transport helicopters to land.

A pair of Wiesel 1s belonging to 5th Company, *Fallschirmjägerbataillon* 272 as seen during Exercise "Certain Shield 91". Note the tactical sign that was used in the early 1990s to identify Wiesel 1-equipped *Fallschirmjäger* units. The Wiesel entered service with *Fallschirmjägerbataillon* 272 in 1990 in order to replace the KraKa. At first all battalions received Wiesel 1s into their heavy companies. During an army structure modification in 1991 that affected the three German airborne brigades that existed at that time, one *Fallschirmjägerbataillon* was converted into an airborne anti-tank battalion (*Fallschirmpanzerabwehrbataillon*) in which all the Wiesel 1s in the brigade were centralized. In *Luftlandebrigade* 27, this was *Fallschirmjägerbataillon* 272, which from 1992 onward bore the name *Fallschirmpanzerabwehrbataillon* 272. Note the periscope on the open commander's hatch.

mobility and reconnaissance capacity after they hit the ground, but with the introduction of the Wiesel 1 weapon carrier these limitations disappeared. On the brigade level, the brigade commander could now either form airborne battle groups, in which an airborne anti-tank company supports an airborne infantry battalion, or use the airborne anti-tank battalion as an independent formation. This formation can be used as a brigade reserve to counter enemy attacks, form strong points by quickly changing powers in the battle to gain the initiative, or operate as a reconnaissance force 15 to 20 km (9 to 12 miles) behind enemy lines. If an enemy armored threat is located by the reconnaissance force, a large number of Wiesel 1s are able to launch a counterattack to slow down the enemy advance and neutralize smaller enemy tank formations.

With a combat weight of 2800 kg (6174 lb) per vehicle, two Wiesel 1s and their crews form the precise payload for a CH-53G. With this load, the helicopter has an operational radius of 450 km (280 miles). Thirty-one helicopter loads are needed to transport all 61 Wiesel 1s of the entire *Fallschirmpanzerabwehrbataillon*, but additional helicopter transport

space is needed to bring in ammunition and support vehicles. All the heavier vehicles of the battalion, including the logistic assets, have to follow on the ground. For moving Wiesels around the world, four can be loaded into a C-160 and inserted into a tactical air landing operation (TALO). If it is not possible to bring in Wiesels by helicopter as an internal load, they can also be carried slung under helicopters.

Wiesels normally deploy with the second wave of an airborne operation after the airborne infantry has secured a helicopter landing site (HLS) to fly them into. If the complete operation is heliborne, it is possible for a mix of troop-transporting and Wiesel-transporting helicopters to land simultaneously. Once in theatre, the Wiesel commanders usually operate along with the infantry, but it is not always easy for them to maintain contact since the Wiesel moves much more quickly than the infantry does.

This rear view of a Wiesel 1 Mk 20mm of 5th Company, *Fallschirmpanzerabwehrbataillon* 262 (which at that time was still officially named *Fallschirmjägerbataillon* 262) clearly shows the fuel tank of the vehicle, which is mounted externally. The self-sealing rubber fuel tank has an explosion retarding polyurethane liner and a capacity of 80 liters (21 gallons). The photo was taken during Exercise "Certain Shield 91".

During the AMF(L) exercise "Alley Express 92" in Turkey, a Wiesel 1 TOW withdraws into a new position after destroying an enemy main battle tank during a fighting withdrawal operation. Note that the crew is wearing German army-issue flak jackets and that the camouflage is made out of foliage. The vehicle belongs to the *Fallschirmjägerbataillon* 263 battle group.

During Exercise "Colibri XXX" in central France in 1992, a Wiesel 1 TOW and a Wiesel 1 Mk 20mm assemble in a helicopter landing site after being brought in by CH-53G transport helicopters. The vehicles belong to *Fallschirmpanzerabwehrbataillon* 283.

Organization of the Airborne Anti-Tank Battalion

At the time of this writing, both German *Luftlandebrigaden* (airborne brigades), 26 and 31, have one *Fallschirmpanzerabwehrbataillon* that uses the Wiesel 1 weapon carrier as their main weapon system. Even though the structure is soon to change, we would like to explain the structure of the current *Fallschirmpanzerabwehrbataillon* before describing the new structure. *Fallpanzerabwehrbataillon* 272, belongs to *Luftlandebrigade* 31, the spearhead of Germany's crisis reaction forces, and is based in Wildeshausen in northern Germany.

Fallschirmpanzerabwehrbataillon 262, based in Merzig in southwestern Germany, forms part of *Luftlandebrigade* 26. Both battalions are equally structured and consist of a HQ, a support company and four combat companies. The latter are structured into the company HQ with the company commander's Wiesel 1 TOW, a Mercedes G wagon as communications platform, the company sergeant major section with a 2-ton and a 5-ton truck and, last but not least, three Wiesel 1 platoons. First and Second platoons are equipped with four Wiesel 1 TOWs and two ammunition supply vehicles based on the Mercedes G wagon. Third platoon is equipped with six Wiesels armed with a 20mm machine cannon and two ammunition supply vehicles. In total, each combat company numbers 57 personnel, and the complete battalion consists of 21 officers, 111 NCOs and 256 enlisted men. Located inside the HQ and support company are all necessary logistic elements, including fuel, food and ammunition supply, as well as a medical asset and a repair and recovery group that can fulfil second line repairs for the equipment of the battalion. In total, the battalion can field 61 Wiesel 1 weapon carriers (4x14 plus 5 for company and battalion commanders) and 138 wheeled vehicles ranging from Mercedes G wagons on 2-ton and 5-ton trucks to 10-ton ammunition trucks and a 13-ton crane.

Two Wiesel 1 TOWs are seen here during Exercise "Colibri XXX" just after they have left the HLS. Note the endless steel wire-lined rubber track. The vehicles belong to *Fallschirmpanzerabwehrbataillon* 283 of the now-disbanded *Luftlandebrigade* 25. During the exercise, 3rd Company supported the paratroopers of *Fallschirmjägerbataillon* 251.

Future Structure of Units Equipped with the Wiesel 1

In the new structure, the *Fallschirmpanzerabwehrbataillon* will no longer exist, and the two airborne brigades will only field two airborne infantry battalions. Inside these so-called *Fallschirmjägerbataillon* there will be a heavy company called *Schwere Fallschirmjägerkompanie*. The

Another Wiesel TOW takes up a defensive position during Exercise "Cold Grouse 95". Note the MG 3 fitted to the vehicle to allow the crewmembers to defend themselves against dismounted troops.

unit will field three platoons, and each will have four Wiesel 1s fitted with the Mk 20mm machine cannon. The fourth platoon will be equipped with four Wiesel 1 TOWs. In addition to these, one more Wiesel 1 TOW will be available in the HQ element of the company for the company commander. The heavy company will also comprise a mortar company equipped with six 120mm mortars. A mortar with a bipod and base plate is currently being used, but once the Wiesel 2 120mm-mortar carrier enters service, the heavy companies will receive the new system.

The Wiesel 1 is not only used in the German airborne forces, but also in the German army's light infantry (*Jäger*) and mountain infantry (*Gebirgsjäger*) units. Inside the two light infantry units (*Jägerbataillon* 292 and *Jägerlehrbataillon* 353) and the four mountain infantry units (*Gebirgsjägerbataillon* 233, *Gebirgsjägerbataillon* 232 *Gebirgsjägerbataillon* 231 and *Gebirgsjägerbataillon* 571), all Wiesel 1s also belong to a heavy company, either the fifth or sixth company. This company can field two platoons of four Wiesel 1 TOWs and two platoons each of the Wiesel 1 Mk 20mm, in addition to two mortar platoons, each with five 120mm mortars on an M-113A2GA2. Each Wiesel 1 platoon fields four vehicles. Like the airborne forces, the mountain infantry and the light infantry will receive the Wiesel 2 120mm-mortar carrier as a replacement for the M-113A2GA2 mortar carrier.

Wiesel Tactics

Usually Wiesel 1s operate in pairs, e.g., one TOW missile vehicle and one 20mm machine cannon vehicle. While the TOW can destroy every known type of armor up to a range of 3750 meters (4100 yards), the 20mm machine cannon is used to engage soft-skinned vehicles and even light armor, as well as dismounted troops and helicopters. Two of these teams often operate together. The Bundeswehr (German army) uses the TOW 2

missile, and it will soon receive the newly designed top-attack FITOW version. The minimum range of a TOW using a HEAT warhead is 65 meters (71 yards). The rocket system is guided to the target by a simple but effective mechanism. While the gunner keeps the target in his sights, the system can track the missile's path because the missile sends out a special infrared signal. If the missile's course needs to be corrected, information is passed to the missile over two command wires.

This Wiesel 1 TOW of *Fallschirmpanzerabwehrbataillon* 272 was photographed during the MND(C) exercise "Cold Grouse 95" in Denmark. During the NATO exercise, the division HQ intensively employed German Wiesels during screening and reconnaissance operations.

During the MND(C) exercise "Cold Grouse 95", a Wiesel 1 TOW vacates the helicopter landing site. The crew is fitting the antennas for the vehicle's radios, which have to be removed for security reasons when the vehicles are loaded into transport helicopters such as the CH-53G seen in the background.

Photographed in the summer of 1996, a Wiesel 1 Mk 20mm of *Jägerbataillon* 292 is deployed to an IFOR helicopter landing site near Gorazde in Bosnia.

The following types of ammunition are available for use with the Mk 20 A1 20mm Rheinmetall machine cannon on the machine cannon version of the Wiesel: high explosive incendiary tracers, hyper high explosive tracers, hypervelocity armor-piercing tracers, and hypervelocity armor-piercing discarding-sabot tracers. The double belt-fed machine cannon allows for a quick change from one ammunition type to the other. Situated on the E6-II-A1 one-man turret are two ammunition boxes that usually contain 60 rounds of armor-piercing ammunition on the left side and 100 rounds of high explosive ammunition on the other. Of course, the combination of one Wiesel 1 TOW and one machine cannon Wiesel 1 Mk 20mm is only one of the many possible options for this highly flexible weapon system.

The big disadvantage of the Wiesel 1 is that it cannot engage targets properly while moving. Therefore, during battle the Wiesel 1 commander usually reconnoiters possible positions where he can take his weapons out of hiding and surprise the enemy. This requires a high level of skill from a possible Wiesel 1 commander who will have to observe the running battle, reconnoiter positions, operate the weapon system, follow the radio, and communicate with his driver, all at the same time. After using the weapons, the crew takes advantage of the Wiesel's high speed and low silhouette to quickly change position, at least 50 meters (55 yards) away from their last one. To prevent early detection by the enemy, positions are both entered and exited from the rear. In a defensive battle, positions are reconnoitered by foot patrols before the vehicles go into battle. During a firefight with

enemy armor, one Wiesel 1 normally changes position while the second observes the battlefield. When both vehicles are operative again, the next target is destroyed. On an all-arms battlefield, the Wiesel 1 will operate together with anti-tank helicopters and mortar fire controllers in order to give the enemy a hard time.

Hidden behind the Wiesel a safe distance from the battle, the two ammunition supply vehicles of the platoon, which are based on Mercedes Benz G wagon, wait to re-supply when ammunition runs short. Seven

This Wiesel 1 Mk 20mm was deployed to the IFOR helicopter landing site in order to provide security for the incoming German CH-53G transport helicopter carrying supplies.

In 1996, parts of *Jägerbataillon* 292 deployed their Wiesels deep into Bosnia in order to provide security for German engineer units who were building a safe road from Gorazde to Sarajevo.

Here the commander of a Wiesel 1 TOW of *Jägerbataillon* 292 from the German/French brigade uses the AN/TAS 4 thermal imaging sight of the TOW to detect suspicious activities. Note the vehicle name "Alex" painted on the tube of the TOW launcher.

The three-man crew of a Wiesel 1 TOW poses with their vehicle in the background and a display of all of their on-board equipment spread out in front of them. Some of the equipment carried inside the Wiesel 1 TOW includes tools for light repairs, recovery equipment, a radio, night vision equipment, tank crew caps, personal weapons, rucksacks, and two TOW missiles. Note that the TOW weapon system has been separated into its main parts. The front plate of the Wiesel has been removed to make the 5-cylinder VW diesel engine visible.

missiles are stored aboard the Wiesel 1 TOW and the machine cannon version carries 400 different types of rounds. Considering the theoretically obtainable rate of fire of 950 rounds per minute, that would not even last for 30 seconds, but usually the 20mm cannon will fire single shots or bursts of three to five rounds.

In addition to its good daytime fighting capabilities, the Wiesel 1 is also fully equipped for night fighting. The two-man crew of the 20mm machine cannon version is equipped with a driver's night sight and a weapon night sight that is effective up to a range of 800 meters (874 yards). In addition to this, one pair of night vision goggles is available. Similarly, the three men of the TOW Wiesel crew have a driver's night sight, a thermal imaging system for the TOW, and a pair of NVGs for the loader. Each Wiesel is also equipped with a PLGR 95PPS GPS receiver that allows the crew to know their exact position at night and in difficult terrain. This is also of great value when fulfilling reconnaissance tasks in unknown terrain during an airborne operation.

Wiesel 1 Development and Operational History

Originally designed by Porsche, the Wiesel is manufactured today by Rheinmetall Land Systems, formally known as MaK *Systemgesellschaft*. The development history of the Wiesel 1 started as early as 1969, when the

German *Bundesamt für Wehrtechnick und Beschaffung* (BWB – army procurement office) started to look for a replacement for its fleet of light, wheeled transport vehicles used by the airborne forces, the so-called KraKa. In the following year, Porsche started conceptual studies for a wheeled and tracked solution. The tactical requirements were adjusted several times to add more details, and in April 1974 the Porsche concept was accepted. By the autumn of 1975, Porsche had been awarded a contract for the production of six sample vehicles of the so-called *Luftlandewaffenträger* (airborne weapon carrier). The first prototype was delivered in October 1976, and in 1977 all six prototypes (three each with Mk 20mm and TOW) underwent extensive trials. The trials were very satisfying, but due to a lack of sufficient funds and structural changes in the *Bundeswehr* in 1979, the project was dropped. In 1981, the search for a replacement of the KraKa started again, and again the tactical and technical requirements were changed several times. In all, the concepts for a new vehicle of nineteen national and international manufacturers were taken into account. In the end, the Porsche concept was accepted. The new tactical requirements were as follows:

Using the TOW anti-tank guided missile system, the Wiesel 1 TOW can destroy all armored fighting vehicles currently in service. The TOW missile, which can be seen here just after it has been launched, has a weight of 28kg (62lb). A well-trained Wiesel 1 TOW crew is able to fire two missiles in one minute. Here a Wiesel 1 TOW of *Fallschirmpanzerabwehrbataillon* 283 engages in live firing at the Bergen Hohne ranges.

During a live firing exercise, a Wiesel 1 TOW commander of *Fallschirmpanzerabwehrbataillon* 272 takes careful aim with the anti-tank weapon system. Note the live TOW missile in the launcher. Each *Fallschirmjäger* Wiesel 1 TOW crew is issued three live missiles per year for training purposes.

The insignia of *Fallschirmpanzerabwehrbataillon 272*, which consists of a parachute and an eagles claw, is seen here painted on one of the unit's Wiesel 1 TOW. The motto of the unit is as follows: *Fest zupacken, nicht loslassen* – Hold on tight and don't let go.

A Wiesel 1 TOW is reloaded with missiles during a field training exercise. The combat load of the Wiesel 1 TOW consists of eight TOW missiles. One is placed in the launcher, six are stored in the rear of the vehicle chassis behind the fuel tank, and the last is strapped on the outside of the rear of the hull. Note that the rear portion of the roof, to which both the commander's and loader's hatches are fitted, can be folded up to allow easier access to the missile storage area.

- All-around ballistic protection;
- Extremely low combat weight, small dimensions and a low silhouette allowing the transportation of two weapon carriers in one CH-53G transport helicopter and on one 10-ton truck;
- High cross-country capability;
- Usability as a platform for the Mk 20mm machine cannon and the TOW anti-tank weapon system, as well as availability of sufficient spare ammunition on board;
- Protection of the crew;
- Use of common components manufactured by the civilian market;
- Air transportability as internal and external loads;
- Low noise emission.

After the release of the new tactical requirements and the availability of sufficient funds, Porsche again was awarded a development contract for an airborne weapon carrier based on the initial development plans. Between March 1986 and September 1987, extensive trials were conducted with the two new prototypes, one fitted with TOW and one fitted with the Mk 20mm machine cannon. After no significant problems emerged, the Wiesel 1 was proved ready for serial production. As Porsche was just responsible for the design, several companies bid for the serial production, and Krupp Mak (which later became MaK *Systemgesellschaft*) was chosen in March 1988.

On 21 December 1988, the BWB signed a contract with the MaK *Systemgesellschaft* for the delivery of 343 Wiesel 1 weapon carriers, 210 of them fitted with the TOW anti-tank weapon system, and 133 armed with the Mk 20mm machine cannon. Delivery began in 1989 and was completed by 1992. Since its introduction, the Wiesel 1 weapon carrier has seen operational action several times, the first time with the German UN troops in Somalia between 1993 and 1994. During that service, Wiesel 1 TOW and Wiesel 1 Mk 20mm performed base-security tasks and provided convoy protection. The Wiesel 1s deployed with the German forces in Croatia in 1995 performed similar tasks. Since then, Wiesel 1 TOW and

In addition to the AN/TAS 4 thermal sight of the TOW and the driver's night vision periscope, the Wiesel 1 TOW crew is also equipped with one pair of night vision goggles for the loader. Here a loader of *Fallschirmpanzerabwehrbataillon 272* poses for the camera while wearing the NVGs.

This is what a Wiesel 1 TOW looks like when it has been prepared for a parachute drop. The dropping of Wiesel 1s by parachute is currently in trials with the German airborne-forces school (*Luftlande und Lufttransportschule*) in Altenstadt. The parachute assembly can be seen on the vehicle. Six 1000kg G 12D SKV-type cargo parachutes are located inside the container bag.

During an exercise, a Wiesel 1 TOW crew prepares their vehicle to be airlifted as an underslung load by a CH-53G transport helicopter. The vehicle belongs to *Fallschirmpanzerabwehrbataillon* 262. Note how the rigging equipment is fixed to the vehicle-lifting points.

A CH-53G carries a Wiesel 1 Mk 20mm of *Fallschirmpanzerabwehrbataillon* 272 as an underslung load. German army doctrine prefers the insertion and extraction of Wiesels by helicopters carrying them as internal loads as this allows the helicopter pilots to fly more tactically than they can with a 2.8-ton load dangling beneath them. However, if necessary a Wiesel 1 can be prepared quickly to be airlifted.

Wiesel 1 Mk 20mm vehicles have been on operations in different parts of the former Yugoslavia. German troops patrolling with IFOR, SFOR and KFOR relied on the Wiesel 1 TOW and Wiesel 1 Mk 20mm as heavy fire support. During this period, the Wiesel 1 saw action in Balkan hot spots such as Gorazde and Mitrovica. At the time of this writing, Wiesel 1s are deployed with the German ISAF contingent to Afghanistan.

Description of the Wiesel 1

The hull of the Wiesel 1 is made out of all-welded steel that provides the crew with protection against 7.62mm small arms ammunition and shell splinters. The engine compartment is situated in the front left of the chassis. Located inside the engine compartment, the power pack consists of a VW 5-cylinder diesel with exhaust turbocharger that provides 64kw at 4500rpm and the ZF3HP 3-speed automatic transmission with six forward gears and two reverse gears. For maintenance purposes, the entire power pack can be changed in about ten minutes thanks to its quick-release connections. The driver's seat is located in the front right, and the driver can enter his position through a roof-mounted single-piece hatch. When driving with the hatch closed, three periscopes provide visibility. The one in the middle can be replaced by a passive night-vision system for night driving. The driver steers the vehicle by means of a small steering wheel. When the parking break is used on one track, the Wiesel 1 is able to turn on one track.

The running gear of the Wiesel 1 consists of three dual road wheels, a track-return roller, a front-drive sprocket, and a rear idler. Over these runs the Diehl Type 622 double-pin track, which has replaced an earlier one made of endless wire-enforced rubber band. A special spring assembly provides track tension. The fighting compartment of the Wiesel 1 is situated at the rear of the chassis.

The Wiesel 1 Mk 20mm is fitted with the E6-II-A1 manually operated one-man turret. Situated in the turret is the 20mm Rheinmetall Mk 20 Rh 202 20mm machine cannon. The cannon is fed via two flexible ammunition supply channels through which the belted ammunition is transferred from the ammo boxes. The left ammo box usually holds 60 rounds, which are normally armor piercing, and the right one holds 100 that are usually HE. A switch box allows the crew to change from one ammunition type to the other. Another 240 20mm rounds can be stored inside the vehicle.

Since the crew of the Wiesel 1 Mk 20mm consists only of the driver and commander, the latter is also the gunner. He reaches his position in the turret via a hatch in the turret roof. The weapon is aimed using the PERI-Z 16 daytime scope or the PERI-Z 59 passive night-vision scope. The turret can be moved 55° to the left and right and the elevation of the machine cannon ranges from −10° to plus +45°. When a TOW anti-tank missile system is used, the launcher is mounted on the roof of the vehicle by means of an elevating pedestal. The launcher can be traversed 45° to the left and right and from -10° to +10° in height. The TOW launcher consists of the traversing unit, the launch tube, the optical sight, missile guidance set, the optical sight, and the AN/TAS 4 thermal imaging sight. The TOW can destroy all known armor at a distance of 65 to 3750 meters (71 to 4100 yards). The rear of the roof of the Wiesel 1 TOW is one large hatch that can be folded to the rear to allow access to the six spare TOW missiles stored horizontally in the rear of the chassis. The two hatches for the commander (on the left) and the loader (on the right) are integrated into the large hatch. The commander and the loader each have two periscopes that

Wiesel 1s usually operate in fire teams of one Wiesel 1 TOW and one Wiesel Mk 20mm. During moving battles, two of these teams operate together. While one fire team is on the move, the other provides any needed cover fire. While the Wiesel 1 TOW is responsible for destroying armor such as main battle tanks or armored personal carriers, the Wiesel 1 Mk 20mm engages light armored vehicles, soft skinned vehicles, and dismounted infantry with its machine cannon. Here a Wiesel 1 fire team of *Jägerbataillon* 371 is seen in position during Exercise "Jäger 98".

A well-camouflaged Wiesel 1 TOW of the fifth, and therefore heavy, company of *Fallschirmjägerbataillon* 373 passes through a village during the brigade exercise "Jäger 98" of *Jägerbrigade* 37. Though its camouflage is out of place in the village, just imagine the vehicle parked along a line of pine trees. With its low hull profile, small size and heavy firepower, the Wiesel 1 TOW can be a real nightmare for tank crews.

allow them limited visibility to the front and side of the vehicle when the hatches are closed. The crew of the Wiesel 1 TOW consists of the driver, loader and commander.

The Evolution from Wiesel 1 to Wiesel 2

The development of the Wiesel 2 chassis began as a private venture of MaK *Systemgesellschaft* during the production of the Wiesel 1 for the German army. The company had discovered that there was a market for other vehicles based on the Wiesel chassis, but which required a greater payload. The first prototype was completed in 1994. In 1996, a 120mm-mortar carrier prototype based on the Wiesel 2 was produced and demonstrated. The mortar carrier is currently in trials with the German army. In 1997, another prototype, the Wiesel 2 ambulance, was manufactured. It underwent user trials in 1998 with the German airborne forces. In 1998, a command and control vehicle prototype left the production plant in Kiel. Other prototypes based on the Wiesel and produced for trials are an engineer reconnaissance vehicle, a reconnaissance vehicle for the airborne reconnaissance company, and an ammunition supply vehicle for the 120mm mortar vehicle. Currently the *Bundeswehr* is conducting user trials with several of these Wiesel 2 variants.

The Wiesel 2 is basically an upgraded Wiesel 1 with a longer chassis, and it will be air-droppable. It can easily be distinguished from the existing Wiesels by a fourth road wheel. Its layout is similar to that of the Wiesel 1 with the power pack situated at the front left and the driver located at the right. The fighting compartment, which is located in the rear of the vehicle,

can be accessed through a large, two-piece door. Inside the Wiesel 2 there is twice as much space compared to the Wiesel 1. Though the Wiesel 2 uses many components of the Wiesel 1, it features a new power pack and transmission, as well as a better suspension system. The following Wiesel 2 variants are currently in trials with the German army:

- Ambulance
- Mortar carrier with 120mm mortar
- Command post vehicle
- Engineer reconnaissance vehicle

During Exercise "Jäger 98", a Wiesel 1 Mk 20mm exits a CH-53G during a heliborne operation. The vehicle belongs to *Jägerbataillon* 371, a light infantry unit.

A well-camouflaged pair of Wiesel 1 TOWs of *Jägerbataillon* 371 withdraw through a wooded area during Exercise "Jäger 98".

This pair of Wiesel 1 TOWs of *Fallschirmpanzerabwehrbataillon* 272 were seen taking part in Exercise "Artful Issue 98" in Sennelager, Germany.

It is said that the *Bundeswehr* has a requirement for 63 Wiesel 2 120mm mortar carriers, 18 Wiesel 2 ambulances, 9 Wiesel 2 command post vehicles, 13 Wiesel 2 ammunition supply vehicles, and 6 Wiesel 2 engineer reconnaissance vehicles. In addition, a new version of the Wiesel 1, the reconnaissance vehicle with the AOZ 2000 surveillance sensor package and a 7.62mm machine gun, is in trials with *Luftlandeaufklärungskompanie* 310.

Also, the development of the Wiesel 1 TOW and Wiesel 1 Mk 20mm is being pushed to be ready for the new challenges faced by the German army. As the original design was made during the last years of the Cold War, one of the main requirements for the Wiesel 1 was that two vehicles would fit in a CH-53G. Therefore, the weight limit was the main concern. Originally, it was not planned to drop the vehicle by parachute, but at the moment the German airborne school in Altenstadt is working on a system that will make it possible in the future to parachute the Wiesel 1 into theatre. This has proved to be no easy task because the suspension of the Wiesel 1 was not constructed to bear the stress of being dropped by parachute and could be damaged by the shock of the impact.

Ozelot – The Short Range Air-Defense System Based on the Wiesel 2

In the early '90s, the German *Bundeswehr* had to adapt itself to new security scenarios, including crisis reaction operations outside NATO territory. It soon became obvious that the German air-defense units lacked an adequate weapon system to defend German airborne or light forces deployed on operations in a remote region against enemy air strikes. To remedy this, the LeFlaSys (*leichtes Flugabwehrsystem* – short-range air-defense system [SHORAD]) was introduced to the German army in 2001.

The tactical and technical request list of the BWB for a light, short-range air-defense system (SHORAD) included the following requirements:
- Capability to destroy enemy aircraft and helicopters (even when hovering behind cover) up to an altitude of 3500 meters (11,480 feet) and a distance of 6000 meters (37.3 miles)
- Identification and tracking of targets up to a distance of 20 km (12.4 miles) and an altitude of 5000 meters (16,405 feet);
- Automatic gathering of information and automatic processing,

A Wiesel 1 Mk 20mm of *Fallschirmpanzerabwehrbataillon* 272 is guided out of a CH-53G transport helicopter by a crewmember during Exercise "Artful Issue 98". Two Wiesel 1s or one Wiesel 1 and a Mercedes G ammunition supply vehicle can be transported inside a CH-53G.

Wearing the German army's armored vehicle crew protective headgear and wind protection goggles, this Wiesel 1 TOW crew member was photographed during the annual MND(C) exercise "Artful Issue 98". Note the MND(C) patch on his left sleeve.

A Wiesel 1 TOW of *Fallschirmpanzerabwehrbataillon* 272 in action during the MND(C) exercise "Artful Issue 98" held in Sennelager training area in Germany. Shown to advantage is the running gear of the vehicle, which consists of three dual road wheels, a track-return roller, a front-drive sprocket, and a rear idler on each side.

transmitting and displaying of this information;
- Interoperability with command and air-defense radar systems of other NATO members;
- Computerized threat analysis and fire control of up to eight fire units;
- Able to operate 24 hours a day and in all types of climate using active and passive sensor technology;
- High mobility, air transportability in transport helicopters such as the CH-53G and suitable armor protection for the crew;
- High degree of automatism ensuring easy handling and short training time for the crew. In addition, small crews were required;
- Low logistic requirements of the system and small service life costs.

In 1993, the German BWB invited several companies in the defense industry to deliver their conceptual studies for the future German SHORAD. The results of the studies were ready by January 1994, and after a tough competition, the STN ATLAS ELEKTRONIK concept was accepted. In the meantime, STN ATLAS ELEKTRONIK had teamed up with Wegmann & Co. GmbH, which today forms part of Krauss-Maffai Wegmann GmbH & Co. KG.

The contract for delivering prototypes was signed in July 1995 and two prototypes, one launcher vehicle and one radar and fire control vehicle, were manufactured. The requested tactical and technical

Photographed in 1998 in Slovenia, this Wiesel 1 Mk 20mm belongs to the heavy company of *Gebirgsjägerbataillon* 571. The vehicle is covering the route of an Austrian aid convoy during the AMF(L) exercise "Co-operative Adventure Exchange 98". Note the AMF(L) badge next to the tactical sign on the front plate of the vehicle.

Well-camouflaged Wiesel 1 TOWs of *Fallschirmpanzerabwehrbataillon* 272 are seen during Exercise "Artful Issue 98" in Germany. The red markings identify the vehicles as OPFOR troops. The AN/TAS –4 is visible above the optical sight of the TOW.

capabilities were proved by Ozelot, as the system was now called, during the extensive user trials conducted between 1995 and 1998. They included the first live firing of the weapon system in October 1997. In June 1998, the German Ministry of Defense placed an order for the first batch of LeFlaSys Ozelot vehicles. The first vehicles of the system were delivered to the German army in early 2001, and the official into-service ceremony took place on 27 June 2001.

LeFlaSys System Numbers, Units and Distribution

The LeFlaSys consists of five different vehicles: The Wiesel 2-based launcher called Ozelot, the Wiesel 2-based radar surveillance and fire control vehicle, the Wiesel 2-based battery command and air-defense co-ordination cell vehicle, the Mercedes Benz MB 300 GD-based interface vehicle, and the Mercedes Benz MB 290 GDT-based workshop vehicle. When the production of the first order is completed in 2003, the German army will have received the following numbers and types of vehicles of the LeFlaSys:
- 50x Ozelot launcher vehicles;
- 10x radar and fire control vehicles;
- 7x battery command and air-defense co-ordination cell vehicles;
- 4x interface vehicles;
- 12x workshop vehicles.

Once all systems are delivered, the LeFlaSys Ozelot will be fielded by three light air-defense batteries, namely *Leichte Flugabwehrraketenbatterie* 100, *Leichte Flugabwehrraketenbatterie* 300 and *Leichte Flugabwehrraketenlehrbatterie* 610. Each unit will consist of three air-defense platoons with five launchers and one radar fire-control vehicle each. In addition, the battery will field one interface vehicle, four workshop vehicles and two battery command and air-defense co-ordination cell vehicles. The German army will use the remaining vehicles for training purposes at the *Heeresflugabwehrschule* (army air-defense school) in Lutjenburg on the coast of the Baltic Sea.

This Wiesel 1 TOW crew belonging to *Gebirgsjägerbataillon* 233 posed for the camera during the NATO exercise "Strong Resolve 98" in Northern Norway. The crew of the Wiesel 1 TOW consists of three soldiers – the driver, the commander seated to the left of the TOW system and the loader on the right.

order to stop enemy aircraft from penetrating into friendly territory. Another option is the deployment of launcher units along a line of communication to protect marching troops against enemy air attacks. In this scenario, it is also possible for a moving Ozelot launcher vehicle to track an enemy aircraft while moving, then stop and engage the enemy once it reaches a suitable firing position.

Here a mixed column of Wiesel 1 Mk 20mm and Wiesel 1 TOW vehicles from the heavy company of *Gebirgsjägerbataillon* 571 advance down a road during the AMF(L) exercise "Co-operative Adventure Exchange 98" held in Slovenia. Due to the cramped conditions inside the Wiesel 1, the crews regularly ride with open hatches, even in ice cold weather conditions when they simply don warm clothing. Note the AMF(L) badge next to the unit's tactical side on the front of the vehicle.

Tactically, the batteries will use the LeFlaSys either to provide object protection or to provide air defense for forces at the forward line of their own troops. Forming an air-defense ring around an objective such as a bridge or an airfield will fulfill the first task. This ring can either be close to the objective or at a further distance depending on the tactical situation. In the second case, the fire units are deployed to form a defensive line in

This photo, also taken during the NATO exercise "Strong Resolve 98" in Northern Norway, shows a Wiesel 1 MK 20mm of *Gebirgsjägerbataillon* 233 that is providing cover at a bridge during an AMF(L) counterattack. *Gebirgsjägerbataillon* 233 forms an integral part of this NATO immediate reaction force.

Seen in Norway in 1998, this Wiesel 1 TOW crewmember provides a good example of the crews' appearance in the field. Under the cap worn by armored vehicle crews he wears a woolen ski mask to protect him against the environment. Other clothing includes a cold weather protection jacket, a GoreTex jacket, and a winter camouflage jacket.

This Wiesel 1 Mk 20mm of *Gebirgsjägerbataillon* 233 painted in winter camouflage sits in position somewhere in the Alps. The vehicle has been lifted by helicopter into this defensive position, which is situated at an altitude of more than 2000 meters (6562 feet).

LeFlaSys Launcher Unit

Together with the radar unit, the launcher unit forms a key part of the LeFlaSys. Both vehicles are based on the Wiesel 2 chassis. The weapon system, which is produced by STN ATLAS and called ASRAD, is mounted in the rear of the vehicle. It consists of the pedestal, which is erectable and adjustable in 360° azimuth and −10° to +70° elevation; the sensor and electronic unit with thermal imaging system; a laser range finder; a line-of-sight stabilization unit; a TV camera; a video tracker unit; and two multi-launch units for two SAMs each. The launcher can be elevated and traversed with a speed of 56° per second. The complete

The operational radius of the Wiesel is limited, but in a location like the Alps where no movement other than by foot is possible, a 20mm cannon is a hard match for an attacker.

launcher and sensor unit has a weight of 320 kg (706 lb).

The launcher was designed to fire the Stinger Block B SAM, but with the help of an adapter, the SA 16 IGLA can be used as well. For autonomous operation, the launcher is fitted with a passive infrared air-defense alert device (IRST – *Infrarot Rundsuchsystem*), which can be operated either from the vehicle or dismounted up to a distance of 30 meters (33 yards) from the vehicle. LeFlaSys can be operated from inside the vehicle or from a distance of up to 50 meters (55 yards) with the use of a cable-linked remote control unit. In both cases, the control unit is the same, and it can be removed from the vehicle by simply unfastening some quick-release clips. In addition, for emergency situations or to boost the firepower, a shoulder launcher for the Stinger is carried on the vehicle. With a SEM 90 and SEM 93, both VHF, the launcher is linked to the radar, surveillance and fire control vehicle, as well as to the battery command post and the interface vehicle.

The crew of the launcher vehicle consists of the driver and the commander, who also operates the launcher unit. For easier navigation, the launcher vehicle is fitted with a hybrid TALIN 3000 navigation system made by Honeywell and a PLGRAN-PSN 11 GPS receiver made by Rockwell Collins. For fighting under NBC conditions and in extreme climates, the battery command and air-defense co-ordination cell vehicle is fitted with an NBC protection system, an engine-independent heating system, and an air conditioning system. For self-defense, a 7.62mm MG 3 machine gun is mounted on the hull and four smoke dischargers are fitted to the front of the vehicle.

A mixed column of Wiesel 1 TOWs and Wiesel 1 Mk 20s is on the move during Exercise "Colibri 36" in southern France. The vehicles belong to *Fallschirmpanzerabwehrbataillon* 262. Note that the AN/TAS 4 on the Wiesel 1 TOW is fitted to the TOW weapon system.

During the German-French airborne exercise "Colibri 36" held in 1998, a Wiesel 1 TOW leaves a C-160 Transall transport aircraft during a TALO (Tactical Air Landing Operation). In total, four Wiesel 1s can be carried inside the C-160 Transall of the *Bundesluftwaffe*. Inside the C-130 Hercules, which is not flown by the German armed forces, there is enough space for six Wiesel 1s.

There is adequate space inside a C-160 Transall for four Wiesel 1s. Here a Wiesel 1 Mk 20mm is being driven into the aircraft, where the crew will soon start to secure the vehicle against moving in order to prevent the load from sliding dangerously during the flight.

LeFlaSys Battery Command and Air-Defense Co-ordination Cell Vehicles

Each battery has two battery-command and air-defense co-ordination cell vehicles that are used by the battery commander and his staff to co-ordinate the fire units and command the battery. One of the two Wiesel 2s operates as a battery command post while the second acts as a link between the brigade/task force air-defense co-ordination cell and the battery. Each of the vehicles is fitted with a SEM 93 for exchanging the relevant information and encrypted data on the air-defense communication net that links the battery command in the air-defense co-ordination cell vehicles with the radar, surveillance and fire control vehicle and the interface vehicle. An SEM 90 inside the vehicles is used for voice communication. The total crew of the vehicle is three soldiers. For fighting under NBC conditions and in extreme climates, the battery command and air-defense co-ordination cell vehicle is fitted with an NBC protection system, an engine-independent heating system, and an air conditioning system. For self-defense, a 7.62mm MG 3 machine gun is mounted on the hull and four smoke dischargers are located at the front of the vehicle. To allow easier navigation, a GPS system is mounted in the vehicle.

LeFlaSys Radar, Surveillance and Fire Control Vehicle

The radar, surveillance and fire control vehicle, which like the launcher is based on the Wiesel 2 chassis, is the central command element of an air-defense platoon. Its mission is to detect and identify targets, conduct threat analysis, select the priority targets, and transmit the target data to the launcher vehicles, up to eight of which can be controlled by one radar, surveillance and fire control vehicle. The key element of the vehicle is the HARD (Helicopter and Airplane Radio Detection) radar system. The radar is able to detect aircraft up to a distance of 20 km (12.4 miles) and to an altitude of 5000 meters (16,405 feet). The X-Band 3-D radar is able to track 20 targets simultaneously and can identify whether the target is a helicopter or a fixed-wing aircraft. An IFF system (Mode 1, 2, 3A, and 4MK-X-A and encrypted Mk XII) allows the quick identification of enemy aircraft. The central element of the radar, surveillance and fire control vehicle is a high-availability computer system with a 64 Bit Intel

One of the main missions of the Wiesel 1 weapon carrier is to support the lightly equipped paratroopers with its heavy weapons. Here a Wiesel 1 TOW commander is discussing a defensive plan with a platoon commander from the paratroopers.

During live firing training at the French Mourmelone training areas, a Wiesel 1 Mk 20mm of *Jägerbataillon* 292 of the German-French brigade takes up a position near a similarly armed French VAB (4x4) wheeled APC.

architecture, in which all data is processed and which is operated from two user terminals inside the vehicle.

Five SEM 93s and one SEM 90 radio make possible the communication between the launcher units and the radar, surveillance and fire control vehicle. A special antenna switch system (INTAS) enables the

A field refueling of Wiesel 1 can be done either with jerry cans dropped by parachute or brought in by helicopters, or from tankers of the HQ and service company at a field refueling station. Less than one hour is needed to re-fill a complete *Fallschirmpanzerabwehrbataillon* with its Wiesel 1s at a field refueling station with four tankers. Here a Wiesel 1 TOW takes on fuel. Eighty liters (21 gallons) of diesel can be stored in its rear-mounted tank. This amount of fuel will allow the vehicle to cover up to 300 km (186 miles).

crew to process the complete communication over two transmitting antennas and one receiving antenna. The crew of the vehicle consists of the driver and commander, who are both trained to operate the radar and radio equipment in the vehicle. Like the launcher vehicle, the radar, surveillance and fire control vehicle is fitted with a hybrid TALIN 3000 navigation system made by Honeywell and a PLGRAN-PSN 11 GPS receiver made by Rockwell Collins. For fighting under NBC conditions and in extreme climates, the battery command and air-defense co-ordination cell vehicle is fitted with an NBC protection system, an engine-independent heating system, and an air conditioning system. For self-defense, a 7.62mm MG 3 machine gun is mounted on the hull and four smoke dischargers are situated at the front of the vehicle.

Conclusion

With the introduction of the Wiesel 1 and the first Wiesel 2 variants, the German airborne forces have received a highly capable vehicle that provides them with armored protection and a longer operational range once deployed on the ground. The Wiesel enables the German paratroopers to increase their offensive capability and their ability to fight a moving battle much more effectively than before. In addition, the Wiesel has proved to be the ideal vehicle for peace-support operations. With its small dimensions, it can often reach places where other armored vehicles have difficulty going. Another positive aspect is that it does not possess as much fear-creating potential as main battle tanks, and therefore proves to be ideal in the de-escalation phase of a peace-support operation when troops work hard to restore normality to a nation's streets.

The patron animal of the vehicle, the Wiesel (weasel), is a small, clever carnivore that is an expert hunter. True to this image, the Wiesel vehicle range is one made up of small, well-designed vehicles whose weapons can be a nightmare for the enemy.

A Wiesel 1 Mk 20mm commander reloads the ammunition box of his vehicle with blank ammunition during an exercise. In addition to the olive-colored 20mm x 139 DM 78 AT 03 blank ammunition, the following types of ammunition are available for the 20mm machine cannon: DM 81 AT 74 high explosive (yellow), DM 43 A1 AT 49/51 tracer (cream white), DM 88 AT 05 target practice training (light blue), DM 48 AT 03 target practice training (light blue), and DM 63 AT 52/53 armor piercing (black).

Each Wiesel 1 TOW platoon has two ammunition vehicles based on the Mercedes G wagon. Eight additional missiles are stored on the ammunition vehicle, each one with a weight of 28 kg (62 lb). The missiles are stored on a special rack with four drawers, each holding two missiles. The ammunition vehicle usually follows the Wiesel 1 TOW closely in battle to keep reloading time to a minimum.

Technical Data for the Wiesel 1

	Wiesel Machine Cannon	Wiesel TOW
Crew	2 (driver and commander)	3 (driver, loader and commander)
Weight	2800 kg	2800 kg
Length	3.55 m	3.31 m
Width	1.82 m	1.82 m
Height	1.83 m	1.90 m
Ground clearance	30.2 cm	30.2 cm
Track width	200 mm	200 mm
Maximum road speed	75 km/h	75 km/h
Gradient	60%	60%
Side slope	30%	30%
Engine	VW 5-cylinder diesel with exhaust turbocharger that provides 64kw at 4500rpm	VW 5-cylinder diesel with exhaust turbocharger that provides 64kw at 4500rpm
Transmission	ZF3HP 3-speed automatic transmission with six forward and two reverse gears	ZF3HP 3-speed automatic transmission with six forward and two reverse gears
Fuel capacity	80 liters	80 liters
Cruising range	300 km	300 km
Armament	20mm Rheinmetall MK20 RH202	TOW
Optics	PERI-Z 16 day sight and PERI-Z 59 night sight	Optical sight and AN/TAS 4 thermal imaging system
Ammunition	400 rounds	8 missiles
NBC Protection system	None	None

A Wiesel 1 of *Fallschirmpanzerabwehrbataillon* 272 patrols the old part of the city of Prisren in Kosovo at the end of June 1999. The Wiesel 1, like the TOW version shown here, proved to be ideal for patrolling the narrow streets of the so-called gypsy village, which was a frequent target for Albanian attacks. Other advantages of the Wiesel 1 TOW during this operation were the AN/TAS 4 thermal imaging sight, which enabled the crews to spot hostile activities at night, and the silently running engine, which sounds more like an engine in a car rather than that of an armored vehicle. The pictured Wiesel 1 TOW is on sentry duty at the Serb church in downtown Prisren.

Also photographed in Prisren in June 1999, this Wiesel 1 Mk 20mm of *Fallschirmpanzerabwehrbataillon* 272 is on patrol in the old city center. Note that the crew is wearing berets and headsets rather than the armored vehicle crew caps, a common practice among the paratroopers who say that the black armored vehicle crew caps look too much like those worn in the Russian army.

A pair of Wiesel 1s from *Fallschirmpanzerabwehrbataillon* 272 patrols in the old city of Prisren. The lead vehicle is a Wiesel 1 TOW which is followed by a Wiesel 1 Mk 20mm. When the Wiesel 1 TOW was originally introduced, it was not armed with a weapon for close defense or to engage infantry. However, troops soon began to mount 7.62mm MG 3 machine guns on makeshift mounts for self-defense purposes, like on the Wiesel 1 TOW in this picture, a practice that was also seen among the troops operating in Kosovo.

Wiesel 1 TOW and Wiesel 1 Mk 20mm vehicles were part of the German KFOR contingent from the beginning of the operation in June 1999. In March 2000, *Fallschirmjägerbataillon* 373 provided the vehicles. When unrest between Serbs and Albanians broke out in Mitrovica, the paratroopers deployed with their Wiesel 1s to the riot-shaken city. Here one of two Wiesel 1 Mk 20mm vehicles and two "Fuchs" wheeled armored personnel carriers deploy on the northern bridge. The Serb part of the city is visible in the distance. Note the skull-and-crossbones badge painted on the ammunition box on the right side of the vehicle.

Another Wiesel Mk 20mm of *Fallschirmjägerbataillon* 373 sits on the northern bridge in Mitrovica in March 2000. The painted "547" identifies the vehicle as one belonging to the 5th Company's 4th platoon. The "7" is the vehicle number. The Wiesel 1 Mk 20s in the 3rd platoon are numbered 1 through 4 and those in the 4th platoon are numbered 5 through 8. Since at that time *Fallschirmjägerbataillon* 373 belonged not to an airborne brigade but to the light infantry brigade *Jägerbrigade* 37, its structure was similar to light infantry units with a heavy company, namely 5th Company. This could field two mortar platoons with five 120mm mortars each, two Wiesel 1 TOW platoons with four vehicles each, and two Wiesel 1 Mk 20mm vehicles with four vehicles each.

After being brought in by a British CH-47D Chinook helicopter, the commander's Wiesel of *Fallschirmpanzerabwehrbataillon* 272 leaves the HLS during the MND(C) exercise "Artfull Issue 2000".

This Wiesel 1 TOW of *Fallschirmpanzerabwehrbataillon* 272 shows the common practice of storing equipment such as rucksacks outside the vehicle. Note the mounted MG 3 machine gun and that the vehicle's crew is wearing flak jackets. This photo was taken in the Netherlands during Exercise "Artful Issue 2000".

This close-up shows the unit-made machine gun mount for the 7.62mm MG 3 on a Wiesel 1 TOW, which provides the vehicle's crew with firepower against dismounted troops. The vehicle, which belongs to *Fallschirmpanzerabwehrbataillon* 272, took part in the MND (C) exercise "Artful Issue 2000" in Belgium.

A Wiesel 1 patrol in the city of Kabul in early April 2002. Also belonging to the first German ISAF contingent, which was spearheaded by *Fallschirmjägerbataillon* 313, was a platoon of Wiesel 1s of *Fallschirmpanzerabwehrbataillon* 272 that consisted of nine Wiesel 1s.

A mixed patrol of Mercedes G cross-country vehicles and Wiesel 1s heads to the center of Kabul. Among the three Wiesel 1 vehicles, one TOW vehicle and two 20mm Mk 20 versions can be seen. Note that there are different ISAF markings on the vehicles; two simply bear the initials "ISAF" in large letters while the third vehicle has a circular ISAF badge in which the "ISAF" is written in two languages.

Of the nine Wiesel 1s in the German ISAF contingent, three were of the TOW anti-tank guided weapon system (foreground) while the remaining were of the 20mm Mk 20 machine cannon version (background).

1:35 M933 MLRS

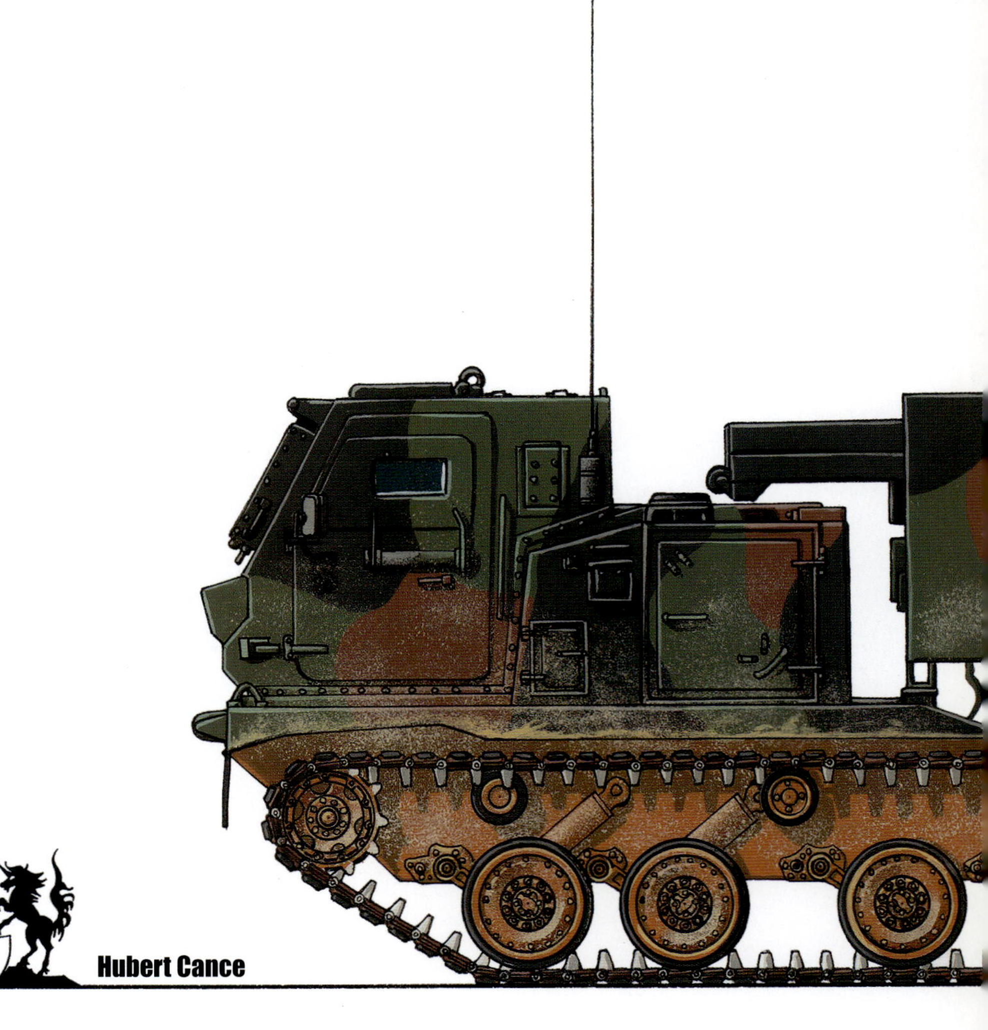

Hubert Cance

Led by a Wiesel 1 Mk 20, a column of Wiesel 1s patrols District 11, the northern outskirts of Kabul. Just like in Kosovo, the Wiesel 1 proved itself the perfect vehicle for mounted patrols in narrow lanes and rough countryside. It offers the crew armored protection against small arms fire and has a low profile. Its night vision equipment allows it to be used as night, and the minimal noise made by the vehicle's engine allows the appearance of the patrol to be a surprise. Note that the German paratroopers of *Fallschirmpanzerabwehrbataillon* 272 proudly wear their maroon berets instead of the issued armored vehicle protective caps.

A Wiesel 1 20mm Mk 20 and its crew from *Fallschirmpanzerabwehrbataillon* 272 await the order to go out on patrol. The *Bundeswehr* uses their Wiesel 1s in Kabul for mounted patrols in the rural outskirts of the city. The Wiesel 1 is more than well suited to deal with the rough terrain. During the patrol, the Wiesel crews often stop for reconnaissance purposes. The sights of the 20mm cannon and the AN/TAS 4 thermal imaging system of the TOW anti-tank guided missile system are used for observation.

A Weisel 1 20mm Mk 20 of *Fallschirmpanzerabwehrbataillon* 272 on patrol in Kabul. Note that the vehicle bears the unit's eagle's-claw-and-parachute badge, German army tactical sign and ISAF markings. The vehicle commander has his 5.56mm G-36 assault rifle ready in case the vehicle is ambushed.

The Wiesel 1 is only issued to the *Bundeswehr* armed with the TOW anti-tank missile system and the Mk 20mm machine cannon. However, the German defense industry tested various weapons on the Wiesel 1 chassis. Shown in 1999 during a live firing demonstration at the infantry school in Hammelburg, this Wiesel 1 chassis is fitted with a 30mm RMK recoilless automatic cannon developed by Mauser.

The *Fallschirmjäger Lehr- und Versuchskompanie* 909 (test and development unit) is also equipped with both variants of the Wiesel 1. Here a Wiesel 1 Mk 20mm of the unit is being used for basic gunner training during which the gunner learns how to properly set the sight on the target. A G-3 assault rifle is mounted coaxially to the 20mm cannon in a system called *Schießarm*. With the use of a special target, the gunner can be trained at a 25-meter (27.3-yard) range using cheap 7.62mm ammunition instead of expensive 20mm rounds.

Another Wiesel 1 version is fitted with a HOT anti-tank guided-missile system and a 20mm machine cannon. The Euromissile-designed weapon system also features a mast-mounted stabilized sensor pod with a TV camera, thermal imaging sight, and a laser range finder. At the time of this writing, the system has not passed beyond the prototype stage. This vehicle is part of a demonstration of the *Luftlandbrigade* 26 in the summer of 2000. In 1997, Euromissile also built a prototype based on the Wiesel 1 of the HOT/ATM (Anti-tank Module) that consisted of two HOT launchers, but lacking the machine cannon.

The Wiesel ambulance was manufactured in 1997 by MaK *Systemgesellschaft*. It is believed that the German army will order a total of 18 Wiesel 2 ambulances to equip its airborne troops with an airmobile and armored vehicle for the evacuation of wounded soldiers from the battlefield. The ambulance vehicle has a combat weight of 4.1 tons, so a CH-53G transport helicopter can transport only one of them. This one is shown during its service in 1998 during Exercise "Artful Issue 98".

The rear view of the Wiesel 2 ambulance prototype. The photograph was taken during Exercise "Artful Issue 98" in Sennelager, when the vehicle was in trials under field conditions with *Luftlandebrigade* 31. Note the vehicle's large rear door that can be opened both to the left and right. It also allows easy access to the rear compartment that can transport one stretcher with one reclining wounded and two sitting wounded.

Technical Data for the Wiesel 2 Variants

	Wiesel 2 Command Post Vehicle	**Wiesel 2 Ambulance**
Weight	3900 kg	3900 kg
Length	4.23 m	4.18 m
Width	1.82 m	1.82 m
Height	2.11 m	1.72 m
Ground clearance	300 mm	300 mm
Track width	1620 mm	1620 mm
Maximum road speed	70 km/h	70 km/h
Gradient	60%	60%
Side slope	30%	30%
Engine	VW 1.9l TDi/AFN that develops 81kw at 4150rpm	VW 1.9l TDi/AFN that develops 81kw at 4150rpm
Transmission	4 HP 240 automatic transmission (ZF)	4 HP 240 automatic transmission (ZF)
Cruising range	400 km (40% cross country and 60% road)	400 km (40% cross country and 60% road)
Armament	MG3 machine gun, caliber 7.62mm; 4x76mm smoke grenade dischargers	None
Capability	Fitted with various communication and command equipment	Transport of one wounded on stretcher and two wounded sitting
Fording capability	Up to 500 mm	Up to 500 mm

`The front view of the Wiesel 2 120mm mortar carrier prototype. The mortar is not visible as it is in the horizontal travelling position. The vehicle has a crew of three soldiers – the driver, commander and loader. In the German airborne forces, the vehicle will replace the Mercedes G as the transport for the mortar sections. In the light infantry and mountain infantry, the Wiesel 2 120mm mortar carrier will replace the M-113 A2 mortar carrier. The *Bundeswehr* is expected to buy 63 Wiesel 2 120mm mortar carriers.

This rear view of a Wiesel 2 120mm mortar carrier shows the weapon in firing position. The system makes it possible to fire a three-round burst in 20 seconds or conduct intensive fire missions of 18 rounds in three minutes. Clearly visible are the two lowered stabilizers that are needed during firing, as well as the soft-recoil system of the 120mm smoothbore muzzle-loaded mortar. For reloading, the barrel swings forward down through a roof hatch and is loaded inside the vehicle by the crew. It then moves back into the firing position to be fired. This procedure allows the crew to operate the mortar without leaving the protection of the Wiesel 2 120mm-mortar carrier. (Rheinmetall Landsysteme)

In total, LeFlaSys Ozelot uses three different Wiesel 2 variants: the launcher vehicle (*Flugabwehrraketenwaffenträger* Ozelot - FlaRakWaTrg); the radar, surveillance and fire control vehicle (*Aufklärungs-, Führungs- und Feuerleitwiesel* - AFF-Wiesel); and the battery command and air-defense co-ordination cell Wiesel (*Flugabwehrführungswiesel* - FlaFÜWiesel). This view shows a radar, surveillance and fire control vehicle in the distance and a launcher vehicle in the foreground at the Todendorf air-defense ranges.

Also based on the Wiesel 2 chassis is the radar, surveillance and fire control vehicle (*Aufklärungs-, Führungs- und Feuerleitwiesel* - AFF Wiesel). The vehicle is shown here with its HARD radar erected. The radar can identify targets up to a range of 20 kilometers (12.4 miles) and a height of 5000 meters (16,405 feet). It can track up to 20 targets simultaneously and distinguish between fixed-wing aircraft and helicopters.

Technical Data for the Wiesel 2 LeFlaSys Launcher Vehicle

Combat weight	3900 kg (launcher vehicle)
Length	4188 mm (launcher vehicle)
Width	1857 mm (launcher vehicle)
Height	1512 mm with launcher in travelling position, 2547mm in firing position
Crew	2 (launcher vehicle)
Suspension	Torsion bars and hydraulic dampers
Maximum road speed	70 km/h
Gradient	60%
Side slope	30%
Engine	1.9litre 4-cylinder TDI direct-injection diesel engine built by Volkswagen that develops 81KW at 4150rpm
Fuel capacity	120 liters
Transmission	4HP 240 transmission with four forward gear and one reverse gear that are shifted electro-hydraulically
Trench crossing capacity	1.5 m
Fording capacity	500 mm

A LeFlaSys Ozelot in action at the Todendorf air-defense ranges along the German Baltic Sea coast. Using the Stinger Block B missile, the LeFlaSys is capable of destroying approaching enemy aircraft up to a height of 3500 meters (11,484 feet) and up to a distance of 6000 meters (6558 yards). (Rheinmetall Landsysteme)

With four Stinger missiles mounted and the launcher in the ready-to-fire position, this LeFlaSys Ozelot launcher vehicle sits ready for action at the Todendorf air-defense ranges. The pedestal launcher unit of the vehicle can operate at a full 360° and has an elevation from −10° to +70°. The launcher unit comprises the sensor and electronic element, the thermal imaging camera, a laser range finder, a TV camera, a line of sight stabilization unit, an auto tracking unit, and the four launchers. The launcher unit is also fitted with a passive infrared air-defense alert device (IRST – *Infrarot Rundsuchsystem*) made by Thales Optics. The IRST can be operated on the vehicle or be used remotely up to 30 meters (33 yards) away from the vehicle.

This is one of the first Wiesel 2-based launcher vehicles of the SHORAD LeFlaSys to be delivered Note that the launcher is in travelling configuration and that the two members of the vehicle's crew are travelling with hatches open. Visible at the rear of the vehicle is the storage box for four spare missiles.

Another version of the Wiesel 2 vehicle range that is currently being tested by the German army is the Wiesel 2 mobile command post (*Bewegliche BefehlsStelle* Wiesel 2). The radio- and computer-filled vehicle will provide the airborne forces with a quickly operational mobile HQ. The vehicle shown here is the prototype vehicle, which like the ambulance version has a combat weight of 4.1 tons. (Rheinmetall Landsysteme)

One of the many variants of the Wiesel 2 is the engineer reconnaissance vehicle. Inside the vehicle is carried all necessary equipment for locating and creating mine fields, obstacles, river crossing points, etc. In addition, radio equipment and navigation systems that allow the crew to keep in contact with the combat troops are also available. (Rheinmetall Landsysteme)

During the EUROSATORY 2002 defense exhibition, Rhienmetall Landsysteme showed off a prototype of the reconnaissance vehicle version of the Wiesel 1. The equipment in the vehicle includes a thermal imaging camera, laser range finder, vehicle navigation system, and extensive communications equipment that allows the transmission of reconnaissance results without loss of time. The crew of the vehicle will consist of a driver, commander and an additional observer. It is believed that if accepted for service, the vehicle will enter the inventory of the German army's airborne reconnaissance units.

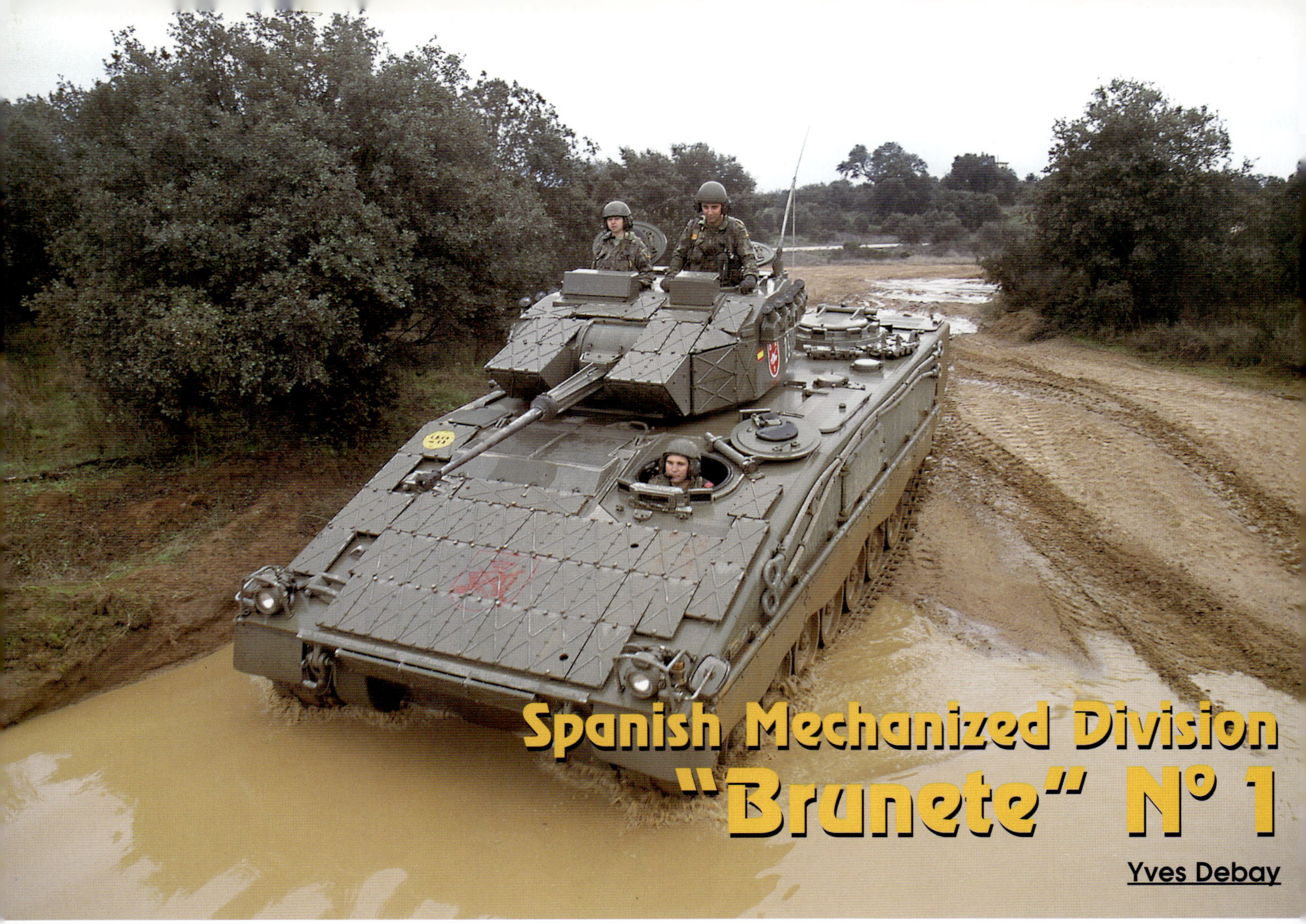

As the Pizarro enters a water hazard at the Sierra Morena Range, the vehicle presents a good view of its additive and reactive armor.

The Biggest Armored Confrontation of the Spanish Civil War

The scarlet badge adorned with a silver tank and the two uppercase letters "D" and "A" (*Division Acorazada* – Armored Division) identifies a vehicle as belonging to Division "Brunete", the spearhead of the *Ejercito*. This great division, which has a tank for its symbol and is named after Brunete, the location of the largest armored conflict of the Spanish Civil War, is the main mechanized unit in the Spanish Army.

Created in 1943 based on the German model, *Division Acorazada* was one of the most modern units of its time. It was equipped with the Panzer IV *Sturmgeschütz* and even a few Tiger tanks, the apex of technology in the 1940s. In the 1950s and '60s, M-47 Pattons and AMX-30s, the most advanced material then in service, replaced the Panzer tanks. The desire to be at the vanguard of progress would never leave the division, which is equipped today with the binomial Leopard 2 and the Pizarro AIFV.

Not only modern technology, but also robustness and Iberian ardor characterize the unit that saw combat action in the Sahara in 1974-74. Today, like all the units in the *Ejercito*, Division "Brunete" is contributing a detachment of troops to Bosnia and Kosovo. Even though the letters "D" and "A" are still present on the their famous insignia, the division has been called "*Mecanizada*" (mechanized) since the vast reorganization of the Spanish army in 1996. Along with the *"Castillejos"* II cavalry brigade, DIMZ "Brunete" N° 1 is part of the heavy component of the Spanish Reaction Force and is also completely integrated into the Eurocorps. Surprise, protection and firepower characterize this mechanized division that is designed for both an effective frontal assault and a solid defense.

Organization

Like any great unit like DIMZ "Brunete" N° 1, the Division includes a command structure, combat elements, and support and logistics units.

The famous badge of Division "Brunete" N° 1.

The tracks of a Leopard 2A4 churn up a cloud of dust during maneuvers at the practice range at Botoa near the Portuguese border.

The command structure is centered on the General Staff of the Division and the Headquarters Battalion. The main fighting force is represented by the following three brigades: Mechanized Infantry Brigade "*Guzman El Bueno*" X, Mechanized Infantry Brigade "*Extremadura*" XI and Armored Infantry Brigade "*Guadarrama*" XII.

Combat support and logistic support are the task of several units grouped within the division structure that the Spanish call the *Nucleo de Tropas Divisionario* (Nucleus of Division Troops).

Headquarters
Based in Burgos in Old Castile since 1997, the Headquarters is naturally the brain and command center of the division. It consists of the commanding general, his staff and the traditional cells attached to the command unit: staffs, information, operations, logistics, finances, civil relations, computer relations, and communication.

This Headquarters is assisted in its task by a Headquarters Battalion (*Batallone del Cuartel General*), which was created in 1997 and includes a staff, a Command and Service Company, Military Police Company N° 1, Intelligence Unit N° 1, NBC Company N° 1, and Music.

The Military Police Company provides escort and security missions and guards the staffs and infrastructure of the Division. It also controls road traffic, handles discipline, and ensures the safe escort of prisoners.

Intelligence Unit N° 1 naturally has a close relationship with the G-2 office of the division staff in charge of security and information. Thanks to its means of listening and detection, notably by ARINE radar, the Intelligence Unit assures the collection, sorting, analysis, and translation of any information concerning enemy activity. The unit is also in constant connection with the Special Forces teams, the allied information services, and the recognition units of the Air Force.

NBC Company N° 1 is the youngest unit in the Division, being created on 10 December 1998. Equipped with a specialized version of the BMR-600 armored personnel carrier, the Company's task is to localize any NBC aggression, study it, mark out the dangerous zones, and possibly ensure decontamination of staffs and materials. The recent affair of the depleted uranium shells in Kosovo required the assistance of specially trained soldiers of the *Ejercito*.

The Leopard 2A4 is one of the most powerful tanks in NATO's arsenal. Two tank battalions in Division "Brunete" N° 1 are equipped with them.

Mechanized Infantry Brigade "Guzman el Bueno" X (BRIMZ X)
The first unit to be officially attached to the Eurocorps (in 1995), BRIMZ "*Guzman el Bueno*" X is a bit of a window into the *Ejercito*.

These Leopard 2A4s belong to Armored Battalion "*Mérida*" IV, which is part of Regiment "*Castilla*" N° 16 of Mechanized Infantry Brigade "*Extremadura*" XI. Based at Botoa, the unit is totally integrated into NATO and could be engaged along with German, Dutch and Danish Leopards anywhere in Europe.

Occupying an area of ground measuring 10,621 acres in Sierra Morena north of Cordoba, BRIMZ X would be the first ones to be issued the new Pizarro armored infantry fighting vehicle (AIFV). The badge of the brigade reminds the viewer that wars in Spain have been dirty and unpleasant affairs. Tasked with defending the fortified town of Tarifa, the valiant knight Guzman "el Bueno" was ordered by the Moors to surrender the town or see his only daughter executed. In response to this threat, he sent them a dagger. A gold medieval castle and a large dagger are now the symbols of the Brigade. Though Leopard tanks and Pizarro AIFVs have replaced the men-at-arms, their spirit remains in the Division.

The Brigade consists of a staff and a Headquarters battalion, notably including Transmission Company N° 10 and Antitank Company N° 10. Its two infantry regiments represent the Strike Force of the Brigade. These units are:
- Mechanized Infantry Regiment "*La Reina*" N° 2, which includes two mechanized battalions, BIMZ "*Lepanto*" II/2 and BIMZ "*Princesa*" 1/2, and
- Mechanized Infantry Regiment "*C- Mech*" N° 10, which includes the mechanized battalion BIMZ "*Almansa*" III/10 and the tank battalion BICCM "*Málaga*" IV/10.

Also part of the Brigade is Field Artillery Group X, which can offer support to the mechanized units with its three batteries of M-109 howitzers.

The Brigade also has *Unidad de Zapadores* 10 (Engineer Company 10) and a logistic group.

Mechanized Infantry Brigade "Extremadura" XI

Similar in concept and organization to BRIMZ X, Mechanized Infantry Brigade "*Extremadura*" XI has been based since the reorganization of the *Ejercito* in 1985 in Botoa, some 25 km (15.5 miles) north of Badajoz. This reorganization, which was probably a bit political, was an attempt to break up the "iron circle" that surrounded Madrid at the time of General Franco when the Division was based in Castile. Times have changed and the Brigade, without forgetting the rich historic pasts of its regiments, is a spearhead unit specializing in modern warfare.

The organization and the means are exactly the same as those of BRIMZ X. Only the names of the regiment change, but in Spain, glorious historic references are omnipresent.

BRIMZ XI consists of the following units: Staff and Battalion Headquarters, Service Company, Transmissions Unit N° 11, and Antitank

Here we see one of the 44 Leopard 2A4s that belong to Armored Battalion "*Mérida*" IV. The very visible division badge on the turret would likely be camouflaged in actual combat.

This nice view of a Spanish Leopard 2A4 shows off the standard NATO three-color camouflage. The *Ejercito* has taken delivery from Germany of 108 Leopard 2A4s taken from the *Bundeswehr* stockpile.

Along with the Leopard 2A4s, Spain will also build under license 200 Leopard 2A5s.

Company N° 11. The latter, like in all mechanized brigades, consists of three platoons of four M-113 TOW.

The combat units are meant to form three mechanized tactical groups and one armored unit. The main combat units are:
- Mechanized Infantry Regiment *"Saboya"* N° 6 '*El Terror*', which contains two mechanized battalions: BIMZ *"Cantabria"* 1/6 and BIMZ *"Las Navas"* II/6.
- Mechanized Infantry Regiment *"Castilla"* N° 16 '*El Heroe*', which contains Mechanized Battalion *"Alcantara"* III/16 and Armored Infantry Regiment *"Mérida"* IV/16.

Field Artillery Group XI of the Brigade has three batteries of eight M-109A5 self-propelled howitzers. The Brigade also includes a traditional company of engineers, *Unidad de Zapadores* 11, and a logistics group.

This brigade has not yet received the Pizarro AIFV, so it is transported in M-113 APCs. On the other hand, a large number of Leopard 2A4s are present in its tank battalion.

Armored Infantry Brigade "Guadarrama" XII
Based at El Goloso at the foot of the Sierra Guadarrama, *Brigada de Infanteria Acorazada "Guadarrama"* XII is somewhat the native unit of Madrid because its 1100-acre base of operation is situated not far from Escurial. Having received its baptism of fire in the Sahara in 1974, BRIAC XII is, according to the Spanish description, the armored infantry brigade

A Spanish Leopard 2A4 from Armored Battalion *"Mérida"* IV travels at full speed along a road at the Botoa range.

of the *Ejercito*. It armament consists mainly of 88 M-60A3 TTS tanks, 259 M113s of various versions, and 24 M-109A5 howitzers. This brigade will doubtless receive the first Leopard 2E (Spanish version of the Leopard 2A5).

BRIAC XII consists of a staff and a traditional Headquarters Battalion, including Transmission Unit N° 12. Unlike the mechanized brigades, BRIAC XII has no anti-tank company. The following units make up the remainder of the Brigade:
- Mechanized Infantry Regiment *"Asturias"* N° 31 '*El Congrejo*', which was raised in 1703 and consists today of a staff and Mechanized Infantry Battalion *"Covadonga* I"
- Armored Infantry Regiment *"Alcázar de Toledo"* N° 61, which consists of a staff and two armored infantry battalions: *"Wad Ras* II" and *"Leon* III"
- Field Artillery Group XII
- Logistics Group XII, and
- Engineer Unit N° 12. This latter unit, just like in the mechanized brigades, consists of three platoons of M-113 VCZ (*Vehículo de Zapadores Combate* – Combat Engineer Vehicle).

Regiment of Armored Light Cavalry "Villaviciosa" N° 14
The origins of *Regimiento de Caballería Ligero Acorazado "Villaviciosa"* (RCLAC) N° 14 are based on the *Tercio de Dragones de Steenhuysen* formed in Flanders in 1689. The Regiment is tasked with using its ability to move rapidly to conduct reconnaissance for the Division during offensive operations and to employ delaying tactics during defensive operations. Life in the Spanish Cavalry, which is a unique and special group, is not always easy. Fortunately, the Regiment is capable of unleashing some solid firepower that has good stopping ability.

The RCLAC *"Villaviciosa"* is composed of a staff, a command squadron and two battalions (*grupo*): one of light armored cavalry (GCLAC) and one of mechanized cavalry (GCMZ).

The GCLAC consists of a staff and three light armored squadrons (ELAC), which include three sections of five VEC TC-25s and two M-60A3 tanks, as well as a heavy mortar section that uses four M-113, three of which carry 120mm mortars.

The GCMZ consists of a staff, a squadron of 13 M-60 tanks, and a mechanized squadron of 18 M-113s dispersed among three sections. One anti-tank section uses BMR TOW and MILAN, which will soon be replaced by Pizarro TOW vehicles. Another heavy mortar section is similar to the one found in the ELAC.

Field Artillery Regiment N° 11
Quartered in barracks at the *"Cid Campeador"* military base near

As Leopard 2A4s roll down a road, a number of M-113 A1 tracked personnel and equipment carriers wait off to the side until called to duty.

Burgos, Field Artillery Regiment N° 11 is the descendent of the Royal Artillery of Spain created in 1710, which became famous on a number of battlefields. Today it consists of a command battery, an objective acquiring battery and two field artillery battalions. Each battalion fields a command battery and two batteries of 16 203mm M-110 guns. This makes for some very serious firepower, especially if it is combined with the 155mm guns attached to the Brigades and the multiple rocket launchers, 203mm howitzers and Santa Barbara 155/52 towed guns that can be detached from Field Artillery Command for the benefit of the Division.

Antiaircraft Artillery Regiment N° 82

Regimiento de Artillería Antiaérea (RAAA) N° 82 provides a protective umbrella so that enemy aircraft cannot interfere in the actions of Mechanized Division "Brunete" N° 1. To complete this duty, the Regiment has a staff, a light battalion of AA artillery, which is formed of three batteries of nine Bofors 40/70 modernized antiaircraft guns, and a missile battery armed with Mistral missile launchers.

This arsenal may seem a little light compared to the firepower of the artillery, but the purchase of more updated antiaircraft weapons is prohibited for budgetary reasons. Fortunately, the presence of a Mistral battery seems to be a deterrent to any air strikes that could hinder the operation of the magnificent Leopard 2E and the Pizarro.

Engineer Regiment N° 1

Based at *Castrillo del Val* near Burgos, *Regimiento de Ingenerios* N° 1 facilitates and supports the movement of the Division. Clearing space for movement, destroying or creating obstacles, and clearing mines are the daily tasks of the *zapadores* (pioneers) of the Division. The Regiment is able to carry out their duties with the help of a staff, an office of engineers, and a combat battalion. The combat battalion consists of a command and service company and three combat companies of armored engineers that mainly use M-113s and other various engineer vehicles and machines.

The Spanish have developed several engineer machines based on the M-60 frame, including the *Zapadores Carro* (tank with a backhoe attachment) and a folding bridge-tank that is fitted with a German Leguan

A Leopard 2A4 tank commander, in this case a sergeant, poses for the camera. Note the subdued unit badge above his left chest pocket.

The crew of an M-113A1 TOW operates their anti-tank weapon with camouflaged faces. They belong to Antitank Company N° 11, which is comprised of three platoons of four vehicles each.

Both Mechanized Infantry Brigades "*Extremadura*" XI and "*Guzman el Bueno*" X have anti-tank companies mounted on TOW M-113s.

bridge. This brilliant battalion has also arranged nine mine throwers on an M-548 frame.

Transmission Regiment N° 1

Charged with communications, *Regimiento de Transmisiions* N° 1 is comprised of a staff, a transmission center operating directly for the division staff, and two signal companies for the zone. A support company supports the whole group.

Division Logistics Group N° 1

We end this portion of the article discussing the *Agrupacithis portion of the artic* N° 1 (AGLD), a real logistic brigade that comprises different units without which combat would be impossible. To recover a damaged tank under fire, drag it, repair it, and send it back to the front, is one of the multiple tasks that falls to these logisticians who are often forgotten by the general public.

To conclude, Mechanized Division "Brunete" N° 1 is simply 17,678 Spanish soldiers using sophisticated materials in the service of Europe, for, let us remember, the Division is attached to Eurocorps.

Main Materials of DIMZ "Brunete" N° 1

207 tanks — 88 Leopard 2A4 and 119 M-60A3 TTS
316 Pizarro AIFV
933 M-113 APC and variants (M-577, M-548)
48 VEC TC-25
105 self-propelled howitzers (M-109A5 and M-110A2)
48 Mistral
27 Bofors AA 40/70mm
104 engineer vehicles (18 of which are bridge layer tanks)
50 TOW launchers
96 Milan launchers
966 heavy vehicles
1544 light vehicles

Pizarro AIFV

In 1984, the *Ejercito* expressed a need to acquire the latest generation AIFV capable of replacing its M-113 and, on certain missions, the BMR-600. The Austrian Steyr-Daimler-Puch group and the national Santa Barbara firm combined their talents to develop the ASCOD fighting vehicle. Based on the brilliant results obtained by the Spanish-Austrian prototype, the Spanish Ministry of Defense ordered 366 models of the vehicle in the infantry version. Sixty percent of the vehicle, which is called the "Pizarro", would be built in Spain. The plan would be for the Pizarro to equip the mechanized units of the *Ejercito* for a period of 25 years. On their part, the Austrian land forces would adopt the vehicle under the name of "Uhlan".

The first unit to receive the new AIFV is the RIMZ "*CThe fi*" N° 10. In the near future, the Pizarro will equip the five mechanized infantry regiments of Division "Brunete" N° 1 and probably certain cavalry units.

There is a plan for developing for the *Ejercito* a diverse family of PC, antitank, mortar carrier, antiaircraft, and ambulance vehicles.

Main Characteristics

Crew: Ten, including the commander, driver, gunner, and seven soldiers
Weight in fighting order: 28 tons
Length: 6.173 meters (20.25 feet)
Width: 2.84 meters (9.3 feet)
Height: 2.55 meters (8.4 feet)

Apart from the TOW antitank weapon, this M-113 is armed with a 12.7mm machine gun for the protection of the crewmembers.

An M-109A5 self-propelled howitzer from an artillery battery belonging to the artillery battalion from BRIMZ "*Extremadura*" XI is directed into position.

Speed: 75 km/h (46.5 mph)
Acceleration: 0 to 50 km/h (0 to 31 mph) in 20 seconds
Engine MTU: Diesel-fed turbo V-8 developing 600 CV
Armament: Mauser 30mm automatic cannon stabilized with a rate of fire of 700 rounds per minute and a coaxial M-3 machine gun. The armament can be used manually or with the assistance of a MK-10 computerized firing system from ENOSA.

Armor Plating: 30mm (1.3 inches); Lateral: Additional 14.5mm (.60 inches) of active armor plating possible. Also present is NBC equipment.

System of Classification of Units in the Spanish Army

Traditionally, in the *Ejercito*, Roman and Arabic numerals are alternated in the numbering of units in their order of importance. Divisions and regiments use Arabic figures, for example, DIV "*BRUNETE*" N°1 or *Regimiento Aerotransportable "Isabel Catholica"* 29 (RILAT 29). Brigades are numbered with a Roman numeral, for example, *Brigada de Infantería Acorazada "Guadarraama"* XII. Battalions use a special system of numbering that combines the two types of numbers: an Arabic number to specify the regiment and a Roman numeral to describe the fighting unit's place in the brigade. For example, Mechanized Infantry Battalion "*Cantabria*" I/6 is the first fighting group in Mechanized Infantry Regiment "*Saboya*" N° 6.

Each brigade in the mechanized infantry brigades contains a field artillery *grupo* (battalion).

The artillery battery consists of eight guns, and the *grupo* is made up of three batteries.

Divisions, brigades and shock troops to the level of battalion are named after a famous person or battle from Spanish history or a well-known geographic landmark. The term "*agrupacíon*" is used for logistic brigades or, more generally, for a fighting group the size of a brigade that consists of ground units, such as those sent to the Balkans. The term "*grupo*" (battalion) is used for cavalry and artillery, whereas "*unidad*" (company) is reserved for the Engineers and Special Forces. "*Tercio*" indicates the famous regiments of the Legion and "*banderas*" the battalions in the Legion, as well as the paratroopers of the BRIPAC.

The M-109A5 carries a six-man crew: the driver, commander, two artillerymen, gunner, and the gunner's helper.

An M-548 tracked cargo carrier that is being used to transport ammunition for an infantry regiment of Mechanized Infantry Brigade *"Guzman el Bueno"* X.

The two main 4x4 utility vehicles used in the Spanish army are the Land Rover and Suzuki.

This brand new Pizarro AIFV belongs to BRIMZ *"Guzman el Bueno"* X.

A new Pizarro AIFV from the Mechanized Infantry Regiment *"C5 A ne"* N° 10 presents a demonstration of its mobility at the Sierra Morena range.

A Pizarro of the "*C0 A Pi*" Nº 10 mechanized infantry regiment in action. The unit was the first to put the Pizarro to use. The Spanish army has ordered 463 of the versatile vehicles.

This photograph offers a good side view of the Pizzaro armored infantry fighting vehicle.

A detailed view of the turret of a Pizarro AIFV that shows the arrangement of the smoke grenade launchers.

The 30mm gun on the Pizarro AIFV is stabilized and uses a sophisticated computerized firing system.

This close-up view of the turret and hull of a Pizarro provides a good look at the 30mm gun and the additive armor.

The Pizarro AIFV can carry up to seven soldiers. Here we a number of Spanish soldiers disembark from the interior of the vehicle.

Spanish soldiers take up a position in front of their Pizarro. They are armed with an MG-3 machine gun, an Ameli LMG and an Instalanza rocket launcher.

The standard service rifle carried by the Spanish soldier is the 5.56mm CETME assault rifle.

This VEC TC-25 armored reconnaissance vehicle is used in Armored Light Cavalry Regiment *"Villaviciosa"* N° 14.

This particular Mistral antitank rocket launcher is not used in the Division, but some like it are used in its Antiaircraft Artillery Regiment N° 82.